The Moral Conquest
of Germany

THE
MORAL
CONQUEST
OF GERMANY

By Emil Ludwig

1945

GARDEN CITY, NEW YORK

DOUBLEDAY, DORAN AND CO., INC.

"Some more centuries may have to pass before one can say: it was long ago that the Germans were barbarians." GOETHE

PREFACE

KNOWLEDGE of the German character might have prevented World War II. This is why in this moment of decisions of world importance I once more try to delineate the German national character—as a warning not to try "democracy" in Germany before a period of education. It is both wrong and dangerous to accept a political distinction between Nazis and Germans, as German propaganda would have it. This book offers a case for the guilt of the German nation.

I have attempted before to present the two sides of the German character: in three studies on Bismarck, the Kaiser, and Hindenburg, and in my biographies of Goethe and Beethoven. These two sides I combined in my book *The Germans: Double History of a Nation*. Its publication was three years ahead of public opinion in this country; in 1941 the German problem was hardly recognized as such. In England, where the upper classes had come to know the Germans well— by the bombs from above and by Lord Vansittart's excellent writings from within—the book became much more popular. A bit of the material in that book has meanwhile found its way into writings of other authors, such as Creel, Nizer, Schwarzschild from whom I am now borrowing some details.

I have come forward with practical suggestions on the postwar treatment of Germany in lectures and broadcasts, in articles and pamphlets, before the Committee on Foreign Affairs of the House of Representatives, and before the AMG at Charlottesville. Many of these ideas were widely contested at the time of their appearance, but today most of them have been accepted.

In this book I try to present a picture of the typical German, for the use of both the member of the future Forces of Occupation and the American reader back home. I have done so by a comparison of the victors and the defeated, and I leave to the latter whatever virtues he may have—except one, the capacity for self-government.

My Swiss citizenship—the greatest good luck of my life—makes me independent in dealing with German questions. The Nazis cannot rob me, and I have no intention of living in Germany. Thus I am free from those personal interests which today prompt so many German émigrés to plead for a democratic postwar Germany. These would-be democrats criticized my comments on the German lust for revenge as far back as 1930 (while the Nazis published a book *The Case of Emil Ludwig*).

I frankly admit that I do not believe there are forces in Germany today which might be able to build another republic; I have watched too closely the German boycott of spiritual and intellectual values by German scholars—a boycott which brought about the destruction of the Weimar republic. Moreover, I frankly admit that world peace seems to me to be a greater issue than German prosperity.

I regret that among the numerous critics of the German nation who share my point of view there are few who are interested in the cultural side of the German mind. For thirty years I have tried to disseminate the knowledge of these very treasures. In this book their spirit is offered as the basis for a German postwar education. Their devaluation would serve the world as little as would a dismemberment of Germany.

To my mind the economic conquest of postwar Germany is secondary to its moral conquest—and this moral conquest is definitely possible. But through nothing less than a temporary extinction of German political independence will this all-important moral rebirth of the German nation be accomplished.

EMIL LUDWIG

CONTENTS

Part One

So lordly is the German patriot that he insists he can stand quite on his own. At the same time he arrogates to himself the achievements of every other nation, insisting that they are all descended from himself, or at the very least that they are his collateral relatives.

GOETHE

1 THE GERMAN CHARACTER

NATIONAL CHARACTER is a genuine reality; it is the sum total of the traits which distinguish a nation as a whole—even though some of those traits may be partially or entirely absent in individual members. Few hesitate—aboard a ship, for instance, in a hotel lobby, or on a train—to single out a man from the motley crowd by the mere look of his head, his manner of walking and speaking, and say, "That's an Englishman—or a Mediterranean type—or a Slav." Physiognomy is the symbol of character.

Let us look at the contemporary German and compare him to the American who in 1945, when these lines are read, will have entered Germany. Let us take a man from the Midwest and his opposite number, a man from Central Germany; a man from Iowa and a citizen of Frankfurt am Main. Regional differences may be discounted here; in fact, they are much less than they may seem to the tourist who perhaps thought the Rhine more beautiful, or the Bavarian country-side more *gemütlich,* than Berlin. It is twenty-four hours by train from Munich to Königsberg, only five to Zurich, yet two Germans from these German cities have more in common with each other than the inhabitant of Munich has with the German-speaking Swiss. To the foreigner who wants basic guidance such details are only confusing.

Let us not seek virtues and shortcomings, but rather look at these two men—American and German—as they have come to be through their heritage, their history, and customs, quite aside from their specific personal gifts and the ups and downs of their own lives.

What first strikes the eye is the self-assured bearing of the American, his serene open countenance when he meets you. He is obviously

natural and fearless and makes no pretense. The German, living under a constant strain, first takes the other fellow's measure and in an
instinctive distrust weighs the risks he may run with him and the
advantages he may gain.

Where the American gets his self-assurance from himself, the German gains what self-confidence he has only by sizing up the other
fellow. The American knows his own value, and no one can upset his
judgment on that point; the German's estimate of himself depends
on the other's attitude toward him—he never stops wondering how
people feel about him. Nothing is more German in that respect than
Hitler's perpetual question as to what the world thinks about the
Germans. Since the German does not possess inborn self-assurance, his
education must at least provide him with the exterior marks of self-
confidence. More than any other people Germans constantly worry
about "honor."

So fundamental a quality can develop within a nation only when a
natural predisposition has been cultivated and strengthened by education. For centuries longer than most civilized nations Germans were
denied freedom and had no rights worth speaking of; public life to
them meant giving and taking orders, no more.

The American looks upon the State—and on any other community,
for that matter—as a plane, as it were, on which all live on the same
level, and therefore share their feeling of self-assurance. The ablest
rise and surpass the others in prestige, money, or artistic accomplishments. To the German any community, and first of all the State,
looks like a pyramid. He himself is but one of its stones, supporting
another one and in turn pressing down upon the stone below. The
higher he finds himself in that hierarchy, the better he feels. To catch
a mere glimpse of the master's boots on top—whether the general's,
the boss's, the Führer's, or the Kaiser's—is all he really asks for.

The American will not hesitate to help someone in trouble in a
crowd, in the street, or on a bus; the pioneer life of his forebears has
developed that instinct which today has become a kind of moral tra-

dition. The German, basically no less genial than others, but without any naïve self-assurance and natural dignity, would in a similar situation be hampered by doubts as to the proper thing to do in view of his particular standing.

Hence the lack of any sense of co-operation among Germans. The broken-down car of another motorist stops the American as a matter of course; in Germany the same American, in trouble himself, will rarely get another car to stop and help him. He is likely to run into the same thing in asking his way. "Sorry, I am in a hurry," is the most likely answer. The "law of the pyramid" prohibits active help; in order to give a hand to another fellow, one must step out of one's proper place, and thereby endanger the whole structure of the pyramid.

Such a perpetual strain produces an inner restlessness, which hardly leads to a joyful life. The American habit of basking in the sun for pure enjoyment is completely foreign to the German. Even his pleasure has to be organized on a schedule—heritage from his military service. Following the "law of the wrist watch" people drive from one spot "affording a good view" to another, with lunchtime fixed to the minute. As with everything else, pleasure is a serious business. I remember overhearing a pallid lass of fourteen ask her mother who wanted her to go for a walk: "What lasting values am I to get out of this walk anyhow?"

The American, who has so much bustle about him, is little bothered by inner commotion. Even sitting under a tree in his garden, the German is full of restlessness; he does not stop drawing up plans for the following hour or the coming day—worrying, whether about a business deal, a work of art, or a fight.

The American is wrong in thinking that the general pace of his life is superior to the speed of German efficiency; in Germany, everything being on a rigid time schedule, things are done with comparatively greater speed. In fact, one can often get things done more rapidly in Berlin than in New York City. The Berliner's working intensity is really greater, and since there is less help around than in this country, there also is less no-load work. Working hours are longer, and days off fewer. Since the United States has turned from a debtor to a creditor country, her working speed and intensity have been lowered. No German would, or could afford to, spend half an hour in the barber's chair. "To relax" has no equivalent in the German vocabulary.

Self-assurance makes the American a man easy to get along with compared to the German. If he asks friends to his home after the theater, and it happens to be Sunday, even the well-to-do man takes them to the kitchen for a raid on the icebox; actually this happened at the White House itself during the first years of F.D.R.'s presidency. The German cannot afford any such fun. If his guests are not his equals, if one of them happens to be his superior at the office and another his assistant, he is at once on his dignity—he could not possibly take off his coat and make scrambled eggs in their presence, like the American.

Among the many Americans in big firms and in the highest government agencies that I have seen entering the office of their superiors, I have not seen a single one—no matter how exalted his chief's position—who would straighten his body, or even show any expression of unusual deference. There is simply a firm handshake and the "how do you do" that from the start produce an atmosphere of equality—although the original meaning of that form of greeting is no longer felt. To call each other by first names, to slap each other on the back, to look for the first common chance for a good laugh—all this establishes a basis of mutual confidence, or at least shows a desire for it. People make friends more easily here than they do in Germany; but friendships are also more easily given up.

When two Germans—and this goes not only for Prussians—introduce themselves with a stiff bow from the hips, body bent at about twenty degrees, at the same time rattling off their names, a natural approach is impossible. A painful pause follows, which one of them is likely to shorten with some comment on the weather, put forth in a half-embarrassed, half-challenging tone of voice.

Two Americans who want to do business with each other try to be as smart as possible—smarter, in any case, than the other fellow. Neither gives in if he can help it; for little as money may mean to them, there is always the American love for competition. To be eager for a thing and be shrewd, and yet to remain fair—these tacit laws of sport also regulate American public life. Hence tenacity in negotiations, and generosity in victory! All this is carried on informally: deals involving millions are settled without witnesses or secretaries, with nothing more than a single word, a figure, or a mere nod.

The German who in the three years of his military service has learned how to give orders and how to take them has no sense of such sportsmanship; fair play is the opposite of giving and taking orders. In the course of the past one hundred and thirty years most Germans have spent some part of their lives in uniform. This makes them prone to transfer barrack habits to civilian life, whether it be municipal government or banking, the manner of calling for a bellhop or of dictating to a stenographer. Great-grandfathers who in their day were made to stand at attention, hands on the stripe of their trousers and, afraid of being spoken to, knew how to accept a command instead of an answer. Such an ancestral background keeps similar forms alive even in the twentieth century.

To make a business contract the German needs first of all a meeting, with one man to preside and the others arrayed, according to seniority, in two rows along both sides of a green table. True, the American has his red tape too; he even asks for a signature on each single sheet of a contract, and in many cases for legalization by a notary public and all that. The United States is the only modern country where people have to take an oath before an authority, right hand raised; to the European who for the first time encounters that custom at an American consulate it seems strange, but the point is that all such American formalisms come after the actual agreement itself.

In Germany an agreement which is not signed by the parties is not safe. It was the Germans who about a hundred years ago introduced the written contract to the Far East; previously it was unknown to the Chinese, who made contracts the English way, by verbal agreement.

That general mistrust stems from the lack of self-assurance. A man who owes what self-assurance he has only to his social position and to that dignity of his that he is at any minute so anxious to uphold, a man who never stops watching the other fellow's reactions, such a man cannot possibly expect any sort of mutual confidence to grow. Fear grows instead—an actual awe of orders.

The term "inferiority complex" does not fully express that psychological situation. What is referred to as German arrogance cannot be accounted for by the notorious bumptiousness of embarrassed people. If it could, Germans would feel inferior (and try to "compensate" that feeling) in the presence of foreigners. Only a foreign theoretician who has seen nothing himself of German reality could raise the question whether that nation is mostly insane. What the Germans do have are particular customs and ideals whose extreme consequences appear as insane. There may be scores or hundreds of perverse people within a nation. But a whole nation is no more likely to be "perverse" than to be blind. Nothing is more stupid than to recommend a whole nation to the doctor instead of to an educator. Lawyers endeavor to secure the acquittal of criminals by pleading insanity. On this theory not a single dictator could be held to account.

In the intellectual field, the restlessness of the German finds a grandiose expression in that striving insatiability which one is tempted to call the Gothic element of the German character. Faust is a typically German figure: eternally dissatisfied, he can never find the serenity and gratification life offers—and yet (even in his own crime) he is always in quest of both. *"Der Wanderer,"* a poem made famous by Schubert's music, well represents that unquenchable quest. "Where thou art not," he sings, "there is happiness."

All this is bound to seem strange to the American in Germany. His own romanticism is, as a rule, spent on an hour of moonlight with his girl, an occasional dance, or boat ride. He cannot see how anybody, let alone a whole nation, can seek anything but "happiness." Yet this is the clue to a true understanding of the significant traits of German character. That never-satisfied urge to go farther and farther, that mystical German *Drang* seems simply fantastic to the foreigner—and that is precisely what it is.

That perpetual forward striving is by no means directed primarily toward money. The Germans' relationship to money has nothing to do with American money-mindedness. Neither do the Nazis—who in most respects represent the exaggerated expression of the typical German—look on money as their goal. Power, glory, giving orders, the feeling of being a *Herrenmensch* (a Master)—these are the things the Hitler youth dreams about and for which he gives his life. He does not serve and fight for a bigger bank account, a better home, or a more beautiful car; what he really fights for is a higher place in the pyramid, both within German society and in the society of nations.

With such a disposition the German is seldom as happy a man as his American counterpart; for what he expects is hard to get. To him not money but power means happiness, and therefore his success depends not only on his efficiency but also on his gift to please the higher-ups. A great part of his ambition consists of his willingness to subordinate himself; in short, of obedience. If the American wanting to get ahead does so without much consideration for others, the German never ceases to accommodate himself to people; and this is true in the most important careers.

While an ambitious American can achieve what he wants through his own talents and energies, the German in his pyramid can reach his goal only by patiently carrying the burden above and pressing down upon the persons below. This is hardly the way to create comradeship, and even less self-confidence. Here, too, it becomes clear how innate characteristics gain strength through customs that are

carried on over centuries—that is how the German came to lose more
and more of his self-security.

Thus he often appears more brutal than he really is. Since all norms
are taken from military life in which the whole male citizenry has
participated at some time or other, a harsh military tone is not only
accepted as natural in all circumstances, but actually aspired to as the
very characteristic of manliness. The clerk, the elevator man, the
waiter, or barber—they are all really quite happy in their cringing
and heel clicking. To have a superior he may look at and also speak
to at times gives a kind of satisfaction to the German. *Verboten* is
rarely criticized—most Germans enjoy it; they enjoy the feeling of
belonging to the power above, exactly if and when that power shows
its fist.

The advantages of such civilian discipline are exactitude and punctuality—both prerequisites of military life. Since in Germany military
education has entered the whole body of civilian life, the latter, in
turn, has derived some advantages from it. The working discipline
at the plants of Krupp, Thyssen, and Zeiss is but a continuation of
military drill. (Hence also the exactness of German philologists.) Men
who under threat of severe penalty learn how to shine every uniform
button, to correct the position of every buckle on their tunic, and to
throw up their goose-stepping legs exactly as high as their neighbors'
will later on also be able to do a more exact job in the grinding of
lenses.

Integrity was another virtue to follow in the wake of Prussian militarism. To offer a tip to a German trainman in order to get second-
class accommodation on a third-class ticket would quickly get a
railroad passenger into trouble. But the same integrity can be made to
work in a democratic country too—witness the example of the Swiss
civil servant who is the most honest in the world. In Germany these
virtues often became sheer pedantry; there was pride behind them—
the pride of being a part of the State—which outweighed the man's
greed. Incidentally, these virtues had already deteriorated under
William II.

The American lives in the superlative: he never tires of hearing who are the wealthiest or the greatest men in the country or on earth and which is the biggest or most beautiful thing of all. The German, on the other hand, lives in the comparative. The hierarchic form of his public life makes him notice jealously all the comparative distinctions of height, wealth, and greatness. Alternatively looking up and down, he is continually checking on his own position, and preferably compares himself with the step next to him in the pyramid. This is what gives him pleasure in both the giving and the taking of orders; for everyone does both. The lowest office boy is likely to find someone he can look down upon. Obviously the German pyramid has its foundations in the very soil. To be respected means to be feared; therefore Germans seem never to give up their "at-attention" posture, unless they exchange it for the posture of an officer in command.

The only superlative that interests them is their conviction that they are the best nation in the world. Most nations, of course, feel that way. But American self-confidence is naïve and therefore never offensive; its British equivalent, thanks to English education, is less conspicuous, while the corresponding French trait appears in personal conversation. It was not the unduly high opinion of their own nation that produced a world-wide ill feeling toward the Germans long before Hitler, but rather the aggressive expression of this opinion, especially the mordant insolence of most Berlin people.

This peculiar state of affairs is universal from the army to business life, and even in the liberal professions.

Anybody overhearing the doctor in charge of a German hospital making the round of his wards would think a Prussian field marshal was approaching with his entire staff if it were not for the white uniforms. His loud voice resounding in the hallway, the doctor talks, now jovially, now with somber accents, while a crowd of assistant doctors and nurses, their necks craned toward the great one to catch his orders the better, in amoebaean chants repeat their *"Jawohl, Herr Geheimrat."* When the doctor enters a ward, his piercing glance rests upon a patient, who, seized by awe, tries his best to sit up and thus demonstrate his utter submissiveness. Such a doctor may well be an outstanding surgeon who has saved thousands of human lives, but, being the boss here, he must, according to German etiquette, play the general.

To the American, personal contact is a simple human affair. He meets his fellow man on common human ground. Whether it be a waiter, the man at the gasoline station, or the bus conductor, there is no difference in his natural manner of speech. If he tips, the coin is taken without strain in posture or look. Americans remember well what it feels like to be "down and out," and therefore regard occupational distinctions as something transitory. The German is anxious to obliterate all traces of his social ascent. A German wife does not refer to her husband as a merchant or teacher or doctor; she speaks of him as an industrialist or a *Studienrat* (member of a public educational council), or a *Sanitätsrat* (member of the board of health). The German passion for titles and medals has its origin in the fact that such labels are really able to buy public opinion.

The general wish to give and take orders has led to the brilliant organization of German life, which is watched over by every German as carefully as civil liberties are in other countries. The idea of the social pyramid which, following the pattern of the State pyramid, is imitated by every community, society, and club makes for a perpetual high tension, barring all cordiality among men. I noticed that peculiar tension in times of peace long before World War I; today the American is sure to feel it all the more—in every office, on every bus, and even in an elevator where people look daggers if someone takes up a bit more space than he has a "right" to. The American will find himself drawn into a hundred times as many petty arguments and encounters as he found back home—in using a revolving door, in parking his car, or over his check at a café. The German has so very few civic rights that he stubbornly insists on whatever "rights" seem his at a given moment.

The State is God. And since that deity shows itself only in uniform, the smallest clerk at the post or tax collector's office proudly sports the garb which invests him with authority. This is also the way in which the century-old belief in the infallibility of the General Staff came into being. While the American never tires of criticizing his president, his senator, or his commander, Germans call such criticism "nagging" or "grumbling." Even if the country or the army collapses, as both did in 1918, the German clings to the faith in his deity and exculpates the guilty emperor or field marshal lest the pyramid's structure be endangered. And yet a change for the better in Germany depends on the hope that the nation may at last give up this faith in its own invincibility.

In comparing the average American college youth with a German student at, let us say, Heidelberg, the American will find more scholarship among the Germans, but he will seldom find among them a group of laughing and whistling youngsters of the kind he has so often seen crossing the campus back home. Instead, he will notice that every one of these boys is always on his guard to give precedence to, or answer properly the questions of, his seniors at the university. I still feel uncomfortable calling an American simply "Judge" or "Doctor," because I was so used to saying *"Herr Doktor"* ("Mr. Doctor") in Germany. Without *Herren* there can be no real servants, and without such serfs life does not seem to have much attraction for Germans.

That meticulous German sense of order leads to a pedantry which permeates all public life. On the staircases of a public building, in the waiting room of a pharmacy, or in entering a meeting—everywhere there is always the same doubt showing on every face: "Who is to be placed over whom? Who has to greet whom first?"

Could liberty thrive on such a soil? Power is what the German craves, from the Führer down to the last bank messenger; power—not freedom; and it makes no difference whether it is the power to unleash war, to order around a hundred office clerks, or merely the right to sport a badge which testifies to a man's belonging to the side in power.

Accordingly, public monuments—which are so significant for the characteristics of a nation—always represent might and victory, and never freedom. On public squares the traveler will look in vain for a hero of liberation such as other nations commemorate in bronze and marble—a hero who led his people against its oppressors and may have fallen in the fight. Unknown to most Germans, there stands one lonely monument to Ulrich von Hutten on a deserted castle in Württemberg. There also are a number of monuments to poets, philosophers, and composers—but innumerable bronze kings and generals, each of them putting forward his right leg, unless reining an unruly horse, or leading an imaginary attack across the public square. In front of the White House a bronze statue of Jackson salutes the passers-by: he salutes the people. No similar gesture would be possible on a German monument; there it is the people who do the saluting, not the general.

Freedom is but a myth in Germany. It lives in poetry. Quite correctly it is expressed in a *Lied* known to every German:

> *Freedom which I yearn for,*
> *Which fills up my heart,*
> *Come with all your radiance,*
> *Like an angel's counterpart.*
> *Far from toil and suffering*
> *Of a world oppressed by wars;*
> *You lead your faithful following*
> *In the canopy of stars.*

A clerk at the post office, a railroad employee, the tax collector, or a policeman—to the American these are people who attend to a specific part of public order and management, paid for out of his own pocket to make life easier for him. He regards the man who holds any one of these jobs as a responsible individual—who vindicates that very responsibility by displaying a metal sign with his name on his door or his desk. To my astonishment I have seen such name plates on the desks of the highest civil servants and generals. Whatever its practical use, the name plate seems also to serve as a symbol of basic equality and mutual confidence between two citizens—one of them simply serving, or advising, the other. I was really impressed when I once overheard a man at a clerk's window asking the fellow behind it who was busy writing, "Listen, any spare time this morning?" No German would dare ask such a question.

In America the State is a union of millions of people who have entrusted a few thousands with their administration. In Germany the State is a deity, imperceptible and enthroned above the clouds; every single public employee is an anonymous priest of that invisible god, equipped with olympian powers over its subjects, over their very lives and deaths. Every civil servant is the superior of every citizen— and as a token of that superiority he wears a uniform. In some big private offices doormen and bank messengers sport such coats of many colors in order to feel nearer to the domain of the almighty State.

The policeman is the most dreaded of all representatives of the German State; but in a hidden corner of his soul the German also loves him—exactly because he is dangerous, the way certain women love the "strong man" who makes them tremble with fear. In a way, the German police officer has the function of an anchor amid the storm-raising high tide of public life. Without him the German would feel he was being carried away by the storm.

The tiniest violation of police regulation makes Germans flare up with excitement. They could never muster the patience of the American who waits quietly in line and keeps his peace while the person in front asks questions about a train's schedule instead of just buying a ticket, or when someone at a department store, with no visible intention of buying anything, just asks how much it is. That American patience has never failed to interest me; I cannot help comparing it to the ceaseless fidgets of the German who is eternally getting into arguments.

As long as the German policeman, like a well-armed and helmeted statue, remains in his place he guarantees public order and calm. If a person approaches him, greets him, and asks for information, the great guardian hardly lends his ear to the question, then possibly shoves aside that person to let a car pass, and when he finally is ready to answer he does it with the bullying tone of a barrack command. He is also as likely as not to add, "Repeat what I said!"

The trainman asking for tickets has the bearing of a detective; in fact, his mere appearance makes people somehow feel guilty. Woe to the unfortunate whose ticket is not in order—all the frustrated will to power in the trainman's breast will cut loose and thunder down upon the poor soul's head! Incidents of that kind which I happened to watch as a child still hold their sway over me: I still feel faintly frightened when that elderly twin pair of polite conductors who do the job on American railroads take my ticket and exchange it for a mysterious slip of cardboard.

That incivility of the German public employee is far from being an individual trait of his own character. In his home the same man is probably just as courteous a person as his American counterpart. As long, however, as he represents the State, he must remain aloof; he allows no one to approach him, and feels right only in the armor of his unapproachableness.

Among free people the public instinctively sides with the plain citizen in case of conflict with a government official. In Germany everybody hastens to acknowledge that the official is right—and why shouldn't he be, as he is the representative of the State? His right to forbid is looked upon as a pillar of the established order, and order, at any rate, has precedence over freedom!

As with anything else, Nature herself in Germany is brought into order and marked out. In public parks the lawn is fenced in, and while in this country dogs have to be kept off the grass, in Germany it is the citizen who has to keep off. The citizen must walk on the prescribed path. Neither will the American visitor find fenceless front lawns, for with no fence against either the sidewalk or the neighbor's lawn there might be trespassing.

The numerous *Verboten* signs are really little disliked in Germany —how little was shown in the days of the Weimar republic, when no one thought of removing them. Whereas in America fundamentally everything not expressly forbidden is lawful, Germans consider as unlawful whatever is not permitted explicitly. "It is verboten to leave the door open" plus a penalty fixed for the malefactor is the German equivalent of "Please close the door."

As a customer the German has the satisfaction of being waited on by lackeys; for once he is superior to and stronger than the other fellow. The American salesman or salesgirl says, "May I help you?" His or her German counterpart awkwardly bends over the counter and asks, "How may I serve you?"

To top it all, any German army officer—even in peacetime—has always been able to do as he wanted. As a child I once had to watch my sister forced to step aside by a couple of army officers who felt like walking in the middle of the pavement.

The German's passion for the power and authority of a uniform gets the better even of his greed. The Prussian Junkers who have unleashed so many wars were only partly landowners of wealth; some were poor, or impoverished members of prolific clans. To enable the scion of such a family to join one of the swanky university fraternities, or enroll in the staff officers' school and live there in style, his sisters gave up all hope of social life and saved money by making their own clothes. Seldom before 1890, under the Kaiser, did Junkers intermarry with big business families (sometimes Jewish too) and thus, as people called it, "regild their coat of arms."

Men's relationships to money depend on their differing outlooks on life and on what they want to get from it. Security, that fondest wish of the average American, is no favorite with Germans. The continuous urge of the German toward expansion, his lasting discontent, that

Faustean striving which can be sensed behind all possible masks, make him long for new spheres of power and domination rather than security.

The American enjoys the moment. As a rule he does not save much; he has his life insurance, and often he borrows on it, almost to the limit of its surrender value, and thus leaves little to his heirs. Less of an economizer than the Frenchman, the German saves more of his income than the American. He is very much concerned about his children's education and, with a constant feeling of responsibility toward his offspring, makes all kinds of personal sacrifices for them. Installment buying never really became popular in Germany. To live in comfort, buy another car, and move to a new home every year are not what the German wants. His moments of happiness come when he is able to expand his business on self-made money, and thereby gain a better social standing.

His attitude toward publicity, too, differs widely from that of the American. An efficient German does not want publicity; he wants to please his boss rather than the general public. Movies and the Nazi party have somewhat changed this state of affairs, but not destroyed its basis. To be publicly mentioned as a donor to some charity drive has little attraction for the German; in fact, the majority of such contributions are anonymous. Neither are there those efforts to "sell oneself" that are so common at meetings and dinner parties in this country. The German would rather be called in to his boss and be praised for his work than see his picture in the local paper. In general he will prefer a promotion to a raise in salary. And he will be prouder of an official recognition of his work than of any appreciation on the part of public opinion. No German photographer would think of asking a man in public life to smile. Even a playwright acknowledging the applause of his audience has to put on a serious expression.

But nothing displays so much of the national character as a people's holidays and their moments of nationwide emotion. The German celebrates his king's or his Führer's birthday, but the American has little interest in the birthday of his president. The German commemorates his military victories of yore—the American the declaration of his independence. Elections and sports, the two biggest events of American life, are not public events in Germany. Wars are the true milestones of national history. The birthdays of Goethe or Beethoven are unknown to the masses, but the dates of the great battles are still school holidays after half a century.

Sport has never been really popular in Germany. In this country there is still a tendency to make military drill into a kind of sport, but German sport life has always been militarized. The numerous athletic societies were only a continuation of military service for ex-servicemen no matter how fat these fellows had grown. Gymnastics and shooting —both more widespread in Germany than anywhere else—are recognized as "knightly" sports.

The lack of genuine sportsmanship has prevented the growth of a concept of fair play. As it is, the Germans have neither an adequate word for "fair" nor for "gentleman"; and as they themselves have no use for either of these concepts in their own life, they use, if necessary, the English words for both. The first time I saw an American football team shaking hands with the beaten foe after one of the big games I could scarcely believe my eyes; that kind of thing would merely look ridiculous in Germany. Hence the embarrassing incidents with German champions at the Olympic Games at San Francisco and Amsterdam. In 1914, when the first English prisoners offered to shake hands with the men who had beaten them in battle, the latter withdrew their hands.

Dueling, the most stupid form of "sport" and in reality but a distortion of the medieval ordeal, is supposed to train the personal courage of Germans, but merely breeds arrogance. The Germans regard dueling with sabers as manly and martial—as distinct from a mere game carried on with ball and bat. Together with beer drinking, dueling is at the bottom of the intellectual decay of German universities.

Foreign travel in great measure takes the place of sport in Germany. It is as much the expression of the inner dissatisfaction of the German and his quest for something superior (which he neither knows by name nor is able to describe) as are his military expeditions. If he wants to say something is good for nothing, the German uses a peculiar phrase; he says, *"Das ist nicht weit her* [That's not from far away]." That is, to appear as really precious something has to come from a far-off land. Their eternal restlessness has many times driven the Germans into the wide spaces of the world. Hence their linguistic talents, matched (among nations who speak one of the great languages) only by the Russians.

Here lie new roots of the German will to conquer the world—which for centuries was something like a mystical urge. The Italian campaigns of the German emperors have many motives in common with the Italian travels of German artists. First the Germans crossed the Alps as Vandals and Goths, animal skulls on their heads; later they sported glittering helmets which, still later, gave way to the velvet berets of those Teutonic artists who descended on Italy, palette and brush in hand.

Except for her western regions, Germany is a poor country. Tilling the soil is hard work. With most parts of the country producing no wine, growing only a small variety of fruit, shrouded for days on end in mist, the German people, so imaginative as a whole, had always to be on the move toward more blessed lands, be it for travel or conquest.

The age-old German wish to "have" France suggests the feelings of a man who, standing in his modest garden, peers over the fence at his neighbor's riches. That yearning for the Mediterranean sun was primarily an idealistic movement, but its final expression was war. Whatever conquests the Germans made they always believed they had got not only more but also better land. There is no other case in world history of a ruler taking his very title from the capital of a foreign country—as the German emperors did by calling themselves Roman

Emperors of the Teutonic Nation. Mystical notions rather than the glory of the Holy See or the fame of the residence of Caesars tied these emperors to the city of Rome.

A passionate, perpetual longing for recognition by others forms part of the German will to power, and explains the great role played by "honor" in German history—down to the Nazis.

The English, too, have been lured out of their island mists. But it was the merchant who made their conquests. The navy was sent out afterward to protect the "merchant adventurer." Although their very nature qualified the English for colonization, they transfered full political power only gradually where they had first opened markets; in some parts of their empire they have not yet gone that far. In spite of their efficiency the Germans could not do well in their colonies. Their martial ideals led them to subjugate foreign tribes rather than to bargain with them. They were more interested in raising their streaming banner and in making natives goose-step than they were in their country's balance of trade. When the Germans lost their colonies in 1919, all except one had become a public burden. In the twentieth century no nation that is not itself free can rule people who are not free.

The German idea of the pyramid stood in the way of German world domination—which, as a domination of world markets, might have been possible without wars. Did not the Germans have many gifts besides their military talents? Are they not efficient and indefatigable? It was precisely because they fundamentally are not interested in money and pleasure that they achieved such success in industry and trade.

As it is, they have much in common with Americans in their efficiency and industry. Both share a predilection for standardized merchandise, statistics, and uniformity in their way of life, and both have the same spirit of enterprise. Since the Russians are only now beginning to develop their pioneer spirit, it has been the Germans and the Americans who have led the rest of the world economically in the recent past—which also accounts for the fact that Americans have felt a greater sympathy with Germans than with Frenchmen. Dangerous competition commands a certain respect.

Intuition told the American that no one but the German was a match for his own tenacity and speed. And perhaps the German would really have taken the lead in industry and international trade had it not been for his fixed idea that the world must be conquered by the sword. This indeed made the difference. Surely no American in 1900 could imagine his President saying, "We are the wealthiest and most powerful nation now. Let's conquer Canada or Mexico." The whole country would have said no. The Germans said yes when called upon for conquest.

With the French—the artistic people *par excellence*—Americans share their ideas of individual freedom. With the Germans they have their efficiency in common. British trends are always fenced in by a number of mental reservations. The psychological bonds between modern Russia and America are greater than Americans may think.

Moved by his urge for expansion, the German (no different, after all, from other men in his elementary sentiments) looked for an outlet —a hidden spot which would offer a place of abode to his emotional life.

He could have found that outlet in religion. But the foundations of Christianity were shattered in Germany long before Hitler. The split into two equally strong churches is but one of the reasons for that decay, another being the power Luther allotted to the State; two thirds of the German population thereby accepted what may be called a "personal union" of their Christianity and their State allegiance.

The deepest cause, however, for this state of affairs lies in those age-old heathen tendencies which—as Hitler quite rightly realized— never really left the German national body, and have gained momentum in the course of the past decades so filled with warfare. In 1910 the German magazine *Der Volkserzieher* could publicly declare that "the Christian idea of brotherly love has worked like poison in the German conscience." In the past hundred years hardly ever did a German ruler or statesman enter a church out of genuine piety. The common man has a good ear for such shades of intention, and as everyone in Germany was bent on imitating the highest-ups, that example, too, has been followed by the average German.

Nor could sports give to the German an outlet for his tension, to let him express man's natural instinct for freedom. The lack of play-fulness among Germans is their most distinctive trait when compared with Anglo-Saxons. Their playing has always a tinge of the tragic. They are really fond of tragedy. Their literature contains many great tragedies, but they have no important comedy writer. They do play with their children, but not with each other—as any group of natural people does elsewhere, let us say, on a day in the country. Everything is serious business with them, everything has weight. It was Goethe who said that "the Germans grow heavy over everything."

Taking things so seriously, the German can rarely afford a hobby. Nor can he relax naturally through such exercise and games as he has, for both are rigidly "organized." Approach a group of Germans at play and so many shouting commands assail the ear that one is likely to think a rifle drill is in progress.

But if the German could not really relax in either his church or his games, he found a secret spot for his emotion in family life and in music.

It is an erroneous idea that the German as paterfamilias rules his family with an iron fist like a commanding soldier. The opposite is true. Family life in Germany is far more closely knit than in this country. There are a number of reasons for this. Children are less independent; but they are reared not in fear of their parents but in respect for them. They have better manners than American young-sters. On the other hand, there is little of the good comradeship that prevails in American homes between a father and his children. Yet the German father never ceases to feel responsible for them. He may argue bitterly with his son over the decisive problems of life, but he will nevertheless stick by him and stand up for the boy even if he turns to crime.

The average family spends its evenings and Sundays largely in the enjoyment of music, conversation, and books. In general the German reads more books and fewer magazines than the American. In his family life the German may best be compared to the Slav. In fact, there is a great deal of the Slav in German blood. All these different traits of emotional life have developed what is described by the German word *gemütlich*—an untranslatable term, primarily applied to German home life. Home cooking is definitely good in Germany, and the place in which meals are served is important; the German is fond of outdoor meals in summer.

The American will notice in German family life a prevalence of aesthetic rather than practical elements. He is likely to be amazed by the loyal attachment to the same house, the same garden, and the same old pictures and heirlooms. The German looks at his home from an aesthetic angle; his home means much more to him than a new car. On his desk, or in his living room, the American has pictures of his wife and his children; pictures of parents and grandparents are rare. Germans revere their ancestors, living or deceased, and give the most honored place to their portraits.

It would be improper for a son or daughter to wear white clothes four weeks after a mother's death; to attend a dance would be shocking. Family history is a steady subject of conversation, even among poor people. Marriage is longer thought over and prepared for than in America; hence perhaps the smaller ratio of divorces. All these things are shattered after twelve years of Nazi domination; but in the long run they could not be destroyed.

The German is less of a connoisseur of food than the Frenchman, but he is much superior to the American. He knows nothing of, and would sneer at, the culinary subtleties a simple French workingman takes for granted at his *déjeuner* high up on a scaffolding. Yet the

American drugstore would not do for him. What he needs is plain food, if only one simple dish. The superior cooking abilities of German housewives have alienated the German men from restaurant food. Contrary to his expectation, the American will not find sauerkraut a regular daily dish; at most it is served once a week. But he will see much less canned food than back home.

Beer drinking has become fatal to the Germans. Their preference for that heavy, fattening beverage, which was already popular with the Germanic tribes of old, is most significant. Their passion for that somberly opaque liquid of many ingredients led them once—exactly a hundred years ago—to revolt; a rise in the price of beer was the cause for this only successful German revolution! Wine has never become a widely popular drink, as it has in Italy and France; even in the Rhineland and on the Moselle wine drinking is something of a festive exception, and is, if anywhere, a daily habit only with the people of Baden. Since the German also drinks much less hard liquor than the British or American, he thus relies almost exclusively upon beer. Therefore there is much less intoxication than in America, but more dullness and apathy. A dictator prohibiting beer for a generation could educate the Germans to more easygoing ways, and free them to a certain extent, at least, from their notorious quarrelsomeness.

Germans are seldom free from thoughts of death—which bother them much more than other nations, except perhaps Russia. Clemenceau even went so far as to suggest that the Germans were "infatuated with death." Only the Jews rival them in pious care of the graves of their parents, the celebrating of anniversaries of birthdays and deaths. The American looks upon death as one casts an ill-humored glance at a flickering candle at the end of a long road; to the German, death appears as a huge fire looming in the distance—a glaring beacon he must watch all his life.

Notions of mystical interrelations between love and death, parents and children, are deeply rooted in the old German tribal sentiments.

The German believes in fate, and is therefore willing to make sacrifices for an ideal—for his greatest ideal, which is power, he lays down his life. Each king finds new throngs of young men who are prepared to die for the sake of power.

The German neither knows nor loves liberty. But he tends to build up a dreamland for his fancy. He is not always able to separate that romantic world from reality, and so he is more easily carried away by theatrical performances than other people. Although he dreads the "strong man," he is likely to fall for some hysterical person whom he may clothe with his own romantic dreams; thus we can account for the adoration felt for both William II and Hitler.

But nowhere has the German found so deep and so lasting an outlet for his frustrated daydreams as in poetry and music. It is by no means a coincidence that a people of serfs is at the same time so musical a nation. Had the Germans ever really known liberty, their sense of reality would have prevented them more than it did from their fatal building of castles in the air and their hazy mysticism. At any rate, the strong combination in them of mysticism and realistic thinking explains why this warrior nation came also to be the nation of musicians.

That German music has no place for the music of the battlefield goes to prove how tenaciously and how methodically the Germans have kept these two interests apart. Neither is there much war poetry to be found in their great literature. The only two great men to be called to leadership by the German people themselves in the course of the past five hundred years—Luther and Hitler—have, whatever their distinctions in character and moral value, one thing in common: their relationship to music.

While German statesmen came principally from noble stock, the great German composers have all risen from the common people. German music, Germany's greatest cultural gift to the world, has risen from the very depth of the national substance.

The origins of that music are only partly ecclesiastical; even before

Mozart church influence had diminished. And since it also emancipated itself early from the Italian tradition and accepted but few Slav elements, one must call this music entirely German. As such it represents a historical fact more important and more lasting than all the German emperors and their victories together.

The German's attitude toward family life and his sentiments toward love and death form the fountainhead of German music, which in transcendental accents apprises the world of the currents of a spirit that has also given birth to German philosophy and the genius of Goethe. Why that spirit has never gained an influence on the State— that I have tried to explain in my book *The Germans*. It remains an irony that the world that is battling the Germans borrows from them its airs of victory.

The tension within the German character can also be read in the German faces. "On the German face," so Goethe says, "God's finger is less visible than in the traits of an Italian." Since the Germans, their own prattle about race purity notwithstanding, represent racially the most mixed European stock, they are not easily classified. Differences of physiognomy among them certainly go beyond any mere north-south distinction. There is a vast amount of nonsense about Nazi theories—rendered no less absurd by their high-sounding terms—designed only to veil the fact that the Germans have been subjected to influences, both racial and spiritual, from the four corners of the world, and so have formed a new unity which defies any scientific terminology.

Side by side with such freak faces as the Nazi bosses exhibit to the world today there can still be found a thoughtful, tender expression upon the faces of some German men and women, generally those of more advanced age.

The American youth with his health and strength and his obvious naïveté has no parallel in Germany. No matter how handsome a young German, his lack of natural bearing and ease prevents him from being a match for the American boy. It is by his assurance and initiative that the American soldier gets the better of his equally daring and equally mechanized German enemy. In the long run nations that fought for liberty have throughout history vanquished those who fought for power.

Health and beauty used to be characteristics of German women. Now, both seem almost completely gone, under the impact of two wars and with the marks of war's grief and sorrow. Gone is the German "Gretchen" the American has heard so much about in *Lieder* and so often seen in paintings; even the fashion of plaited hair, re-established at Hitler's order, could not restore the type. The debasement of the German woman to the rank of a breeding machine for future soldiers has left its mark on her and has done away with a certain tenderness which was once typical of German womenfolk.

On the other hand, emotional tragedies have, as it were, dignified the bearing of many older women; some of them seem almost like middle-aged Madonnas. The best-looking faces in Germany were to be found among burghers and peasants rather than among noblemen; it is the beauty of patient suffering.

The idyllic dreams of the German *Frau* appear in hundreds of Lieder and poems. The wish of the German man to be "somebody," which never loses its grip on him, is much less general among German women. In fact, the German woman has at no time incited her man to war; the German Valkyrie never existed after the wars of the ancient Teutons and Goths. But since the German man through centuries has had no influence on public affairs himself, women have felt even less of any such ambition.

This is why German history knows of practically no outstanding woman, be it a queen or a king's mistress. There also are only very few German women artists of importance. While German literature contains not a single great love epic, it has produced the most beautiful love poetry. The Germans have no classical love story in the vein of Tristan, Heloïse, or the poetry of the Brownings. Nor do they have such couples as Dante and Beatrice, Paolo and Francesca, or Madame de Pompadour and her king. Goethe and Frau von Stein are not popular figures. The two heroines of national legend, Brunhild and Kriemhild, are shown as quarreling with each other (being German women, they would) about precedence at the church door.

There is hardly any difference between the German character of eighty years ago and the type which will be found by the armies of occupation. Perhaps the Germans have grown a few degrees ruder and a little more cynical. In any case there is no indication of a sudden change for the better. The lack of an inner balance and self-assurance, that heritage of many generations, has no doubt grown more severe, thanks to the contrast between German pipe dreams and the reality which they now experience—another cruel awakening from their imagined world. Their will to be active cannot have vanished. It is hardly imaginable that a genuine desire for freedom has sprung up over night. But family life, that traditional place of refuge of the Germans, and music, their ancient solace and comfort, are sure, in the long run, to prove indestructible.

The only thing that may have been broken to pieces in many a German heart is the conviction that the Germans are indeed the world's *Herrenvolk*.

From an analysis of German character—we can draw sound conclusions as to how Germany should be treated after defeat. Lack of such knowledge led to many of the psychological mistakes at Versailles.

2 EIGHT GERMAN PORTRAITS

THE FOLLOWING CHARACTER SKETCHES of famous German personages are to be taken as symbols. The selection is only partly accounted for by my personal knowledge; five of these men I have presented in full-length biographies before. Moreover, I had to limit my choice to persons known outside of Germany; some others, no less typical in their lives but known only in Germany, had to be omitted.

These sketches present two men at a time belonging to the same period. Since the present book aims at familiarizing the American reader with the German character as such, the lasting value of what these men accomplished is of less interest here than their personalities, which display varying degrees of "Germanness."

Goethe and Beethoven.

The greatest figure in a thousand years of German culture bears few German traits; but these few are among the best of all German characteristics. In Goethe it was the personality which made his work possible. In fact, Goethe's character is as astonishing as his genius.

Goethe (1749–1832) could not express himself in an artistic medium open to all mankind, such as painting or music. His work is written in a German partly out of use today, and at any rate not to be rendered fully in translation. Only an equally powerful master of creative language could translate his poetry, while his prose requires a subtle knowledge of eighteenth-century German. Both these facts account in some measure for the American impression of bewilderment in Goethe's work. Moreover, not more than fifteen volumes of the hundred and fifty of his original work exist in English translation.

Goethe is the Faustean man—and in this sense he is German. The figure Dr. Faust, magician, savant, traveler, and mystic, served him as a mask to present his own problems. For sixty years he worked on his *Faust*. In parts that national dramatic poem of the Germans bears all the complexity and heaviness of Dante. And the latter parts of his *Wilhelm Meister*, presenting a self-portrait in many different forms, are even more difficult reading.

I feel at this point the urge to essay a condensation of what I have tried to say before in well over a thousand pages.[1]

---

[1] *Goethe, Geschichte eines Menschen* was published completely, in fourteen languages, only the English edition is abbreviated, to about half the original length of the German text, so that the English edition is only a torso.

Goethe's whole life was an indefatigable search for knowledge. It was filled with the desire, if not to unite with Him, at least to come to terms with the Almighty. But that striving never attained its goal in spite of all exertion. For both exertion and striving grew with the years, and only after many an inner trial did Goethe gain the balance he so ardently craved. For many decades he was in search of composure and serenity, but only rarely did he alight, like a royal eagle, upon a lofty peak to survey the land his genius had covered in its flight.

All this seems strange to the American; he is likely to look for leadership in masters who teach him to be happy; that Goethe seldom does. But he leads to far higher forms of human gratification, and shows the way to a late harmony few other men have ever attained.

But there is another facet which may enable the American student to understand Goethe: his pioneer nature, his continuous activity which finds happiness in straining every fiber, to create new energies, gain new vistas. Goethe's diaries all untranslated would certainly astonish Americans with their daily evidence of tremendous activity.

A philosopher and politician, a poet and scientist, an artist and public administrator—to Goethe it was given to convey his message in a hundred different forms, real and fictional. Only as a great savant is he to be comprehended fully—like Leonardo da Vinci, who also in a few paintings hinted at what Goethe has fully put forth in dramas, poems, and novels.

Whatever he said and did served merely to clarify his own inner life. He could not hope to influence his contemporaries. It was only after a century or more that his knowledge was to ripen for the world. He searched nature and art to perfect himself. In all the crises of his life he turned to the creation of verse, which was to lend more beauty to the German language.

The equally productive occupation of this genius with such varied matters as the cultures of antiquity, anatomy, public affairs, and the theater is a typically German phenomenon. It actually compares with the medieval Dr. Faust. Magic and romantic elements combine with a predilection for organization amounting to pedantry—a mixture typical of the German character.

One thing was completely alien to Goethe: the Teutonic will to war—the German lust for fighting. Goethe never fought—not even when his life was in danger, as happened twice. Yet he had a definite feeling for co-operation. As a young cabinet minister during a sudden fire he used to take the lead with the fire bucket himself, and on other occasions he stood for hours in icy water helping with his own hands to protect his town from inundation. He never touched a weapon, except as a young man at an occasional shooting party.

He never tried to justify his nation's faults. Goethe is one of the very rare representatives of cosmopolitism in Germany. An international brotherhood, art, and science meant everything to him—conquest and patriotism nothing. Independent of the judgment of others, he could not be bribed by power. To his prince he said what he felt was the truth, and what he felt should be said. In the face of all Germany he dared to revere Napoleon—until the day before his country's enemy—because he saw in him the one living genius besides himself.

Spending a lifetime at court and joining in whatever flourishes court life required, he still was critical of the nobility; when his duke elevated him to the nobility, he said he hardly knew what to do with his new status. His wife, as did nearly all women who attracted him, came from common stock. His closest friends were commoners.

Beethoven was more ecstatic than Goethe and much less philosophical. "Beyond mortal ken" was the comment of people who listened to his piano improvisations. These improvisations are lost. Of his written works two hundred and fifty-four exist (numbered in one hundred and thirty-five opera).

While Goethe never ceased to study and write for his own personal perfection, Beethoven throughout his life sought perfection in his work. He was no dreamer; he had definite, set goals. His indefatigable activity reminds one of Goethe's; but whereas Goethe mirrored his ego in his work and cared little for power or influence, Beethoven actually set out as if to conquer the world. He, too, never fought physically, but he loved conflict and victory. Like Goethe, he was fascinated by Napoleon—his Third Symphony bears proof of it.

In this half-German, half-Flemish offspring of the proletariat, descendant of singers, lackeys, and cooks, there burned an unquenchable ambition to be the first, the greatest of all men. Knowing, as he did, the eternity of art, the conquest of the universe by music seemed greater to him than conquest by battles.

He first became famous as a pianist. He wanted to travel from country to country, presenting his genius to men by playing, improvising, conducting. When he grew deaf he renounced these dreams, and henceforth expressed himself in his compositions.

Beethoven felt himself to be a world conqueror as strongly as any German emperor ever did. Only four or five of his compositions close in a tragic mood—the others often end in triumph. A fighting, conquering spirit is present everywhere in his music, which rises from sorrow and bewilderment to victory and clarity.

Liberty he has glorified only in two works for the stage, *Fidelio* and *Egmont*. But never did he tire of presenting man in his struggle, and the strain of his craving. Fight and victory are the two perpetual motifs of his work. The great resignation that overshadowed his later life never led him to abandon his feeling for dignity. For due honor he fought with passion—in that respect he was more sensitive than any other composer except Handel, who was his model.

Such ardent desires often drove him to revolutionary outbursts. Defiance was written on his face as it is in his melodies—a defiance which, born from self-confidence, found little or no response. The stormy sky of his unruly nature released the lightning of his themes. In his outer life that disposition brought him into many a tragicomic episode; in his work it enabled him to find new accents for human emotions.

Of the harmony which fills his symphonies and sonatas but little is apparent in his later life. He plunged with violence into the conflicts inevitable between world and genius. He was the archetype of the fighter: manly, fiery, never yielding. In that sense he was more German than Goethe.

But all this took place on a plane far above national issues. Like Goethe, Beethoven regarded himself as belonging to that super-national republic of the spirit whose champions are scattered over the earth. In his core he had no consideration for classes or privileges. But nevertheless he took it amiss if he was not treated like a king. Beethoven was always demanding. Goethe always giving.

Those evenings when Goethe alone in a small room at a Bohemian spa listened to Beethoven's piano improvisations belong to the great moments of German history which will survive all battles. Two majesties recognized each other, and forgot Germany.

Bismarck and William II.

Bismarck (1815–98) is looked upon in this country with both admiration and suspicion. As a historical figure he may remind Americans of Washington: he, too, succeeded in unifying a number of small states under the fire of armed opposition. But while Washington fought an enemy who contested the independence of these states, Bismarck fought against Germans who contested the supremacy of Bismarck's own country. But the urge for unification was similar, and so was the final success.

Moreover, Bismarck's Austro-Prussian War of 1866 may suggest a certain similarity to the Civil War here. What distinguishes these two coinciding conflagrations is the fact that in America one faction forced the other to remain in the Union, whereas in Germany one country compelled the other to secede. There is no analogy between Bismarck's motives on the one hand and Washington's and Lincoln's on the other: America fought for freedom first and then for unity; Bismarck fought for unity in order to get at the helm of the unified country.

There is no better example of both the gifts and the limitations of German statesmanship than Bismarck. His fascinating figure has repeatedly prompted me to present him in both biography and drama. His physical stature, his habit of giving orders, and his contempt for the common man he owed to his Junker ancestors. But he also was the son of his mother, who came from a line of liberal jurists from commoner stock.

He knew quite well that his great mental power came from his mother's side. But exactly because he knew it he was suspicious of that heritage. His mother's enthusiasm for the July Revolution in France was the cause of heated arguments between her and her fifteen-year-old son. When she later removed a portrait of his paternal grandfather from his room, young Bismarck began to hate her—a feeling from which, as he confessed himself, he never freed himself. Although he did not use in the famous form the slogan "blood and iron," without doubt he availed himself of the German lust for war to further his own political purposes. And an anti-democrat he remained throughout his life.

But he, too, was subject to the age-old German qualms. "Man's genius is like a fallen angel, beautiful and sad," he wrote to his fiancée. His, too, had something of Dr. Faustus' ever-searching mind. He was a great reader. In his youth he had a liking for revolutionary poets such as Lord Byron and Schiller. At a comparatively early age he traveled abroad and studied languages and history. All this was not in the Junker style. He developed slowly, because nature anticipated the long life which was to be his. Not before his thirtieth year did he turn to true Christian beliefs—and his "conversion," to be sure, is a complex and confused story. As an octogenarian he still had his moments of Teutonic paganism, as, for instance, when he once said that after his death it would be best to hang him on a huge oak tree and let the sun parch his body.

In contrasting Bismarck's methods and his achievements both the high-handed Prussianism and the more constructive aspects of his life become manifest in all their wealth of ideas. The American student whose forebears gained unity within the short space of twelve years is apt to forget that German unity was essayed in vain for at least seventy years before Bismarck. Keeping this in mind it is easy to see why a man who was domineering by nature reacted as Bismarck did in the face of those previous luckless attempts; one understands how he set out one day by himself, and got what he wanted by defiance and pertinacity and force—methods quite different from those the German people had tried to use before.

Bismarck realized that those previous attempts had hardly ever gone beyond a vacillating trend. He also realized that the Austrian empire, a country with no less than seven non-German national groups besides German-speaking Austrians, could not be included in a German federation, and thus decided to use the best German army to defeat this rival in a *Blitzkrieg,* and exclude him from the union he planned.

But the surprising thing is that this man of violence rose to be a genuine statesman. While the old king and his victorious generals were ready to march to Vienna in 1866, Bismarck alone managed to prevent such a triumphal advance, and forced his sovereign into a generous peace with no territorial or financial sacrifices from Austria. There are certain similarities in that attitude to the way in which the North dealt with the defeated South in this country after the Civil War. Bismarck was also against the annexation of Lorraine after the victory in France some years later—well as he knew there was no one to prevent the new Reich from bagging even half a dozen French departments. But this time he failed to override the generals, flushed with victory.

From that time on Bismarck preserved peace in Europe for the twenty years that he held office. He turned down all temptations to whip France again. He bridled the arrogant lust for conquest which had grown with Germany's growing prosperity. And only at a late stage did he consent to a naval and a colonial program, but not without curtailing both. The old Bismarck proved to be far superior in political wisdom to the aged Frederick the Great: he defied his own caste, even his personal friends, and embarked on social reforms of a kind that this country came to enjoy only fifty years later.

Bismarck knew his Germans, and knew how to make use of their weaknesses. He had a thorough scorn for them, and once reproached them with the lack of what he so aptly termed civic courage. The only two lifelong friends he had were a Baltic Russian and an American, the well-known Mr. Motley. Twice, once as a young man and again as an elderly gentleman, he fell in love: of the two women one was English and the other Russian.

There were fissures in his cragged nature. He was a hypochondriac and suffered from depressions—though not from crying fits, as has been maintained on the evidence of a single case; it was his often watery eyes which made people suspect him of weeping, when in fact his emotion was merely one of contempt.

In the midst of his most successful activities he would turn his back on the world. He seemed completely happy only when alone in his forest, in the company of his wife and his horses and hounds. He found the happiness of momentary relaxation in music and some bottles of wine. Only rarely did people see him laugh, but he had a caustic wit. He loved few men. One morning he said, "I have hated all night long."

He was deeply impressed by Beethoven's music. He must have felt how much he had in common with the composer—the Faustean element, the great question they both were forever asking of God and Death, was as alive in Bismarck as the will to power in Beethoven. Before leaving for the Austro-Prussian War, an orchestra played

Beethoven's Fifth Symphony to Bismarck. Once he said, "Music to me calls forth two heterogeneous feelings: lust for war, and a desire for the idyllic." It is a revealing remark, and better than any other I know describes the German character.

Not before his career drew to its close did his whole pride reveal itself—that pride which he had checked so often before his king, in spite of the latter's evident inferiority.

William II (1859–1940), the grandson and heir of William I, was unintentionally the first to succeed in making the old chancellor a really popular figure. Bismarck's sudden dismissal by the youthful emperor aroused the sympathy of the nation which until then had had as little love for him as he had for them.

But soon the Germans forgot the incident. In the course of the following twenty-five years they grew constantly ever more enraptured by their new taskmaster. That enthusiasm, expanding in wider circles, is one more proof of the typical German weakness for hysterics; the mere sight of such figures appeals to their hazy mysticism. The acclamation of two neurasthenic leaders within the lifetime of one generation (the Kaiser and Hitler) is unique in modern history. Well-balanced individuals and nations look for and find sound leaders. Among American presidents and among English prime ministers there has hardly ever been a nervous man. One need not refer to the unverified gossip concerning the homosexuality of the Kaiser and Hitler to prove their pathological state of mind—their general behavior furnishes ample proof.

Symptoms of decadence have long been present in the Hohenzollern dynasty. In the Kaiser these symptoms were clear from the very first. He was a conceited young man who tried to act the emperor role; he knew little enough, yet never sought information and, endlessly talking, pretended to know everything. His grandiloquence and his irresponsible adventurous actions imperiled his heritage, and lost it.

Added to this was a physical drawback which he tried to conceal instead of admitting it freely, thus winning the people's admiration for his energy. True, his military duties did put certain difficult demands on his crippled left arm, and in my life of the Kaiser I have tried to do justice to his complicated situation. In his own memoirs, written two years later, William as a septuagenarian confessed at last to the world what he had hidden for a lifetime, as if being crippled were a shame.

It was a weakling who took command of the greatest military power of his days. A weakling was soon threatening his neighbors with endless oratory, taunting the great powers, as it were, with a mailed fist. He never stopped clamoring for "recognition"—which the world, in fact, had never withheld from him. That perpetual shifting from threats to complaints by which Hitler later on captivated the Germans and nauseated the outside world, that unquenchable yearning for applause and "honor"—both symptoms of the German lack of self-assurance—contributed greatly to the tension which ultimately led to war.

For twenty years Bismarck had succeeded in preventing war. William II started his war at the least favorable time. At the very last moment he grew panicky and was ready to call it off; but he was surrounded by powers stronger than he. Going off to war, this "war lord"—an ironic term for that hysterical weakling—seems to have felt like a sick man who, on his way to the operating room, has given up all hope. A famous marginal note of his, dating from those fateful days, shows the full extent of his despair.

When disaster finally caught up with him, he followed his true nature and escaped from the country which he could have saved for his dynasty without much exertion. For the German people, including labor, was not and is not republican. There is no other instance in history of such an ignominious flight as that of the twenty-two German kings and ruling princes who in November 1918 fled in such deadly fright from a people that was only too willing to protect them.

Recorded private statements of Bismarck's prove that the very aged man had foreseen both that collapse and the republic. Publicly he declared that any disappearance of the princes would bring about another split of the Reich into the original tribal communities; he overrated the importance of the dynasties and underestimated the German people. The flight of the German ruling princes actually did not harm the unity of the Reich.

In an old snapshot, taken in 1895, the octogenarian Bismarck is to be seen standing up in his carriage to greet the Kaiser, a man of not yet forty, who is approaching on horseback. They both wear army uniform. There is a certain forbearance in this picture of the two men so different in descent, education, age, accomplishments, and personal outlook—a symbol, as it were, of not only what men may grow to be in Germany, but also a symbol of the type of German the Germans themselves most love. They dreaded and certainly never loved the giant Bismarck, because he faced them with natural self-confidence; but they loved the neurasthenic Kaiser, in whose vacillating insecurity they recognized themselves. Millions of them continued to keep their faith in him until his death.

Nietzsche and Wagner.

The least German of all Germans of genius was Friedrich Nietzsche (1844–1900). He himself was so anti-German in his feelings that he came to take refuge in certain Polish ancestors of his by the name of Nietsky. The shape of his head did suggest that of a Slav; but millions of Germans have similar Slav features. He actually was the son of a German pastor, and was born in Central Germany.

His early education was primarily Greek, Italian, and French. And while he loved Greek and Latin culture throughout his life, he mocked at the German philosophers and poets. The only German genius he acknowledged was Goethe—but him he saw not as a German. Nietzsche's ideals were as un-Germanic as were his dogmas; to call him the father of Nazism is ridiculous. His ways of thinking, feeling, and writing were Latin through and through; in his later years he made a conscious style of that Latinism.

Nietzsche was bitterly opposed to democracy. But his was not the high-handed Junker aversion toward popular rule; he was deeply suspicious of the mass as such—any mass. That is why French and English readers may appreciate Nietzsche, but Americans never. The reader must either go through the fire with Nietzsche or burn him therein. He defies all classification.

Even his passionate anti-democratic sentiments failed to bring him nearer to the Germans. Germans, too, believe in an elite—but in a German, or at any rate a Nordic, elite; Nietzsche believed in and turned toward the Latin elite.

This longing for the Mediterranean on the part of a Saxon-born pastor's son is German enough; it is the very same passion which drove both medieval emperors and German artists to Rome. So fond was Nietzsche of Italy that everything there seemed beautiful and great to him, imbued with "divine serenity." A look at Nietzsche's forehead reminds one indeed of a Machiavelli's head or a Leopardi's. No wonder he felt himself a self-chosen citizen of Italy.

His frail physique seems to have been the psychological cause of his admiration for physical strength. Gobineau, his precursor in the idea of a master elite, was of an equally delicate constitution; he could not bear the climate of the very Scandinavians he admired so much. Nietzsche found the strength he needed under the Mediterranean sun or in the highest alpine valleys. There he could walk and climb for hours on end. His best ideas, so he once said, came to him on those walks. Returning home from his walks, he would go to a darkened room and put down his thoughts by the dim light of a kerosene lamp.

Although he glorified war as a symbol, he bitterly criticized the Franco-Prussian War, and was by no means in favor of the new warborn Reich. But he volunteered nonetheless as an army nurse, and with his own hands gave help to the suffering men of this people for whom he had so little love.

Faustean elements were present in Nietzsche too. He gained his balance of mind only through solitude. He lived a secluded life, practically without women or friends. He was like a runner who pushes himself on to ever greater speed; the tension of his never-ceasing imagination mounted to ever greater heights—until, in his middle forties, he collapsed and became insane.

Since his most daring writings date from the two or three years preceding his illness, it has been easy for his adversaries to label them as phantoms of a sick brain. Actually, in that ecstasy his mind climbed to heights never before attained. The brilliant formulation of his epigrams is like hammered silver. And Nietzsche's really seducive prose suggests a dancer of ultimate perfection.

But what he thought of the Germans—who curiously enough fancy themselves to be the elite he had in mind—may be seen from the following quotations:

"Whoever has lived among Germans must count himself fortunate to find one of them who remains aloof from idealistic self-deception and from that color blindness the Germans love and even admire as a virtue. . . . Good-natured, content in small pleasures, lecherous in their dreams, always desirous of being able to discard their innate submissiveness to duty (at least in the theater), submissive to those above, envious of each other, yet deeply self-satisfied in their core . . . the Germans are a dangerous people—they understand the art of poisoning. . . . All true Germans have gone abroad. Present-day Germany is in a pre-Slav stage, and prepares the way for a pan-Slav Europe."

If Nietzsche could not stand the Germans, he is said, nevertheless, to have championed racial purity. Let us listen to him on that score:

"How much mendacity and dull wittedness it takes to pose questions of race in present-day Europe with its mixture of races—provided one does not trace one's descent from Borneo. . . . Wherever races are mixed, there one finds the source of good cultures. Maxim: Never have anything to do with a man who takes part in this mendacious 'race' illusion. . . . As a nation in which races are mixed and stirred up to the greatest extent imaginable (possibly even with a preponderance of pre-Aryan elements), and as a people of the middle in every sense of the word, the Germans are to themselves more incomprehensible, more contradictory, more baffling, and indeed terrifying even to themselves than any other people. They defy definition, and thereby are the despair of Frenchmen. . . . German profundity is often nothing but a halting process of digestion. And since all chronically ill and dyspeptics tend toward comfort, the Germans love 'frankness' and 'simplicity.' How convenient it is to be frank and simple!"

And since Nietzsche has been claimed by the Nazis as their kinsman in anti-Semitism, we cite the following passage:

"To encounter a Jew is a pleasure, especially when one lives among Germans. . . . Undoubtedly the Jews are the strongest, toughest, and purest race of present-day Europe. . . . That the Jews, if they so wanted, could even now gain preponderance in if not mastery over Europe is an obvious fact; it is similarly obvious that they do not plan for and work toward that goal. . . . The fight against Jews has always been the symptom of cowardice, inferiority, and envy; whoever joins that fight must have a good bit of mob spirit in his mind. Now with their steady intermarrying into Europe's best nobility the Jews will soon have come into a fine heritage of spirit and body. . . . Then they will be called the inventors and pathfinders among Europeans."

Contrasted with Nietzsche, *Richard Wagner* (1813–83) appears as German indeed. One is tempted to call him the most dangerous German who ever lived. He represents the actor type among Germans. In his propensity for lying he is akin to his admirer Hitler—but, unlike the latter, he was a real genius. His talent for metamorphosis and his complete lack of any conviction would have qualified him well as a leader of the German people, had the revolution of 1848 in which he took part succeeded and brought him to the helm.

He is indeed the ideal Nazi model. Like the Nazis, he freely mixed folk myth with glittering parades, the bombast of dogmatic slogans with the rattling chorus of warriors. He himself confessed to a purpose beyond aesthetics. He wanted to impress the masses by throwing his heroes and heroines into the screaming paroxysm of mortal combat. With the exception of *Die Meistersinger von Nürnberg* all his operas display fight. His music glorifies a religion of violence. Right is trodden under foot, friends are betrayed and women humiliated. In only one *Tristan und Isolde,* does his genius flower without these philosophical trimmings. That opera is Wagner's chef d'œuvre.

A preliminary list of Nazi crimes reveals a striking similarity to the record of Wagnerian heroes. Wagner's own peculiar language is hardly accessible to the American, even though he may know German well; nor will translation ever succeed in fully rendering the sense of Wagner's original. Quite similarly, Hitler's speeches appear more tolerable in English translation. I once tried to explain to an American who called Hitler's style "simple" how fortunate the reader of the English version is in that respect.

Stripped of its mannered and precious language, Wagner's text reveals the same basic banality as Hitler's. But those turgid exclamations of the *Herrenmensch* Siegfried, of Lohengrin, the messiah, and Hagen, the pallid traitor—these ejaculations have contributed more to German education in the past fifty years than the scholarly writings of a General Bernhardi or the work of the racist H. Stuart Chamberlain. The Hitler youth in the audience of a *Walküre* performance, his eyes glued to the shining sword in the ash tree, instinctively touches his own little dagger, as if vindicated by the romantic example on the stage. In the *Ring* he saw the blond hero, uninhibited master of women, serving poisoned potions and thrusting swords into his fellow man's back; treacherous demigods; cheated giants. Wagner came to be the first educator of a generation that today may still prefer these suggestive Wagnerian images and chants to the sober reality of total war.

The cunning and malice in Wagner's own character—which led

him so easily throughout his life to shift his allegiance from one political party, prince, or nation to another to serve his purpose taught German youngsters a kind of opportunism which encouraged them to renounce what they held to be true whenever it was advantageous to do so.

Effect was the ultimate goal of everything in Wagner. Nothing was sacred to him—neither wedlock nor friendship. Wagner betrayed everyone and everything, in the end even his own *Weltanschauung*.[2]

Wagner's nature, like Luther's and Frederick's, was not harmonious and never sought harmony. This has made all three popular with the Germans, much more so indeed than Goethe. For the uncompleted arch is the German's favorite conception; he loves fragments—loves them even in his own life. The emotional fissure which marks Wagnerian heroes—not excluding Wotan, the world's overlord—is deeply significant of the German world of our days.

In Wagner's work the Germans found all the haziness, the spookish clouds, and somber dreams of the north—and thus they met themselves. Apart from Weber's *Freischütz,* no other German stage figures have so strongly caught and kept popular imagination in Germany as Lohengrin and Siegfried. These heroes appealed to the German's hidden leaning toward a mixture of brutality and naïveté. In them he found that falsification of motives which his nature seems to crave, and which Hitler later on gave him in such perfection: so-called noble motives to justify all misdeeds, world domination under the cloak of world salvation—all this wrapped in an exciting, abstruse-mystical language full of false pomposity, where young warriors rode with streaming pennants and shining armor, virgins not of this earth appeared and were raped in the darkness of mist, sensual outcries full of longing for death and redemption touched the ear, and "death itself and love were locked in each other's arms." Motifs were repeated over and over again—it was the same method which Hitler later on boasted

[2] The author has attempted to present the phenomenon Wagner in his book *Wagner oder die Entzauberten*. 1913.

of when he said the crudest lie grew to be truth through endless repetition.

Before Wagner the Germans had never heard their own legends
presented on the stage by real poets. Faust was the only popular figure
of German saga. As a rule the great dramatists before Wagner preferred foreign subjects. So little popularity indeed did Germanic
mythology enjoy among Germans that the Germans themselves did
not realize the full scope of Wagner's falsifications.

Wagner clad Germanic heroes in bearskins, put animal skulls on
their heads and swords into their fists—and thus created the stage
tradition of what may be called the uniform of the primeval Teuton.
But at the same time he endowed them with all the psychological
complexes of modern times, not excluding an oversexed emotional
life. The Wagnerian world-domination motif tinged the ambition of
the Reich. No other artist has imbued the Germans so deeply with an
urge for world domination as Richard Wagner.

Hitler became literally intoxicated with Wagner's motifs, his stage
characters and the pattern of their lives. He himself confessed to
having received his highest inspiration from Wagner's work. The
perfect Nazi world indeed! *Der Ring des Nibelungen* is about a magic
ring which gives world domination to him who wears it. The whole
affair amounts to a triumph of treachery, bristling with broken oaths
and treason between friends, lovers, children and parents, bondsmen
and masters.

No master can be blamed for what his disciples misread in his work.
But in Wagner's case his German disciples did understand him. The
Nazis fulfilled Wagner's dreams. They imbued the whole nation with
Wagner's creed of force and spite.

Hindenburg and Hitler.

In the year 1806 most of the Prussian fortresses surrendered to the
Napoleonic armies almost before they were attacked. "Prussian forts

can easily be taken by cavalry"—so the emperor wrote home. No less than fourteen commanders of such forts, noblemen most of them, capitulated after mere token fights. Only one of them was condemned to death for cowardice (though pardoned subsequently)—General von Beneckendorff und von Hindenburg, who had yielded the fort of Spandau without firing a shot. This man was the great-uncle of the field marshal who later dropped the "von Beneckendorff" and called himself simply von Hindenburg.

Thus the family von Hindenburg has come to the fore twice in German history: one of its members surrendered a fortress without even attempting a defense, the other did the same with Germany. No further exploits of this Junker family are recorded.

Chance gave Hindenburg his position at the outbreak of the war. The Kaiser was looking for some kind of "titled governess" for General Ludendorff who, though of commoner stock, was looked upon in competent quarters as a great strategist. Von Hindenburg, long retired, unknown in wider circles, not even recalled to active service at the outbreak of the war, seemed a good choice.

With Ludendorff's rise to virtual dictatorship in the latter stage of the war, old Hindenburg also rose to prominence. In fact, all he did in those four years was to sign whatever Ludendorff, nominally under his command, "submitted" to him. He graciously accepted fame and a popularity for which he seemed to be singled out by his full-sounding name, his giant stature, his great mustache, and his taciturnity. Moreover, he was said to have been wounded on the skull in 1866—a fact which also offered a patriotic excuse for what some people considered not the most brilliant of minds. In fact, he never was wounded.

On September 28, 1918, Germany's fate hinged on three men: the Kaiser, Hindenburg, and Ludendorff. The question was whether or not to withdraw into the fatherland and defend it to the last. On that day the three men threw up the sponge; they decided to form a new government which was to offer an armistice "within twenty-four hours." Courageous leaders in such moments usually are ready to pay for their former privileges and accept death rather than dishonor.

The Kaiser, a coward by nature, had no will of his own in that perilous hour. Ludendorff simply resigned. And thus everything was left to the decision of the aged field marshal. Perhaps in that hour as he capitulated he remembered that Spandau ancestor of 1806. The other two fled the country; he stayed. His aides counseled co-operation with the new government—which indeed did not hesitate to collaborate with the defeated generals.

Thus the lone survivor of the old trio grew to be a national hero. Six years later he was elected president of the Reich. He himself professed never to have read any books except military manuals. He also was frank enough to admit his complete lack of any understanding of politics. Convinced royalist though he was, still he took the oath to the republic—no one knows whether he crossed his fingers during that ceremony. Later he publicly supported the much-discussed indemnity payment to the runaway Kaiser, until the bill was adopted, and a hundred and thirty million gold marks were transferred to the royal exile. Slowly Hindenburg began to whittle away the republic with the help of the army officers and Junkers. In the end he ruled practically without parliament.

He despised the "Bohemian corporal," as he called Hitler. But eventually he had to give way to the people's choice, and make its hero who commanded the numerically strongest Reichstag party chancellor of the Reich. As an octogenarian he shifted his allegiance to the swastika—the third flag he had sworn to in his life. He signed all the criminal decrees of his chancellor, not excluding the "legal justification" of the mass murder of June 30, 1934. Shortly after that he died, after turning over virtually all power to Hitler.

The cultural treasures of the nation were unknown to him. One critical remark on Goethe, rather comical, is about the only bond he ever had with German intellectual life. All he really wanted was to destroy the republic and restore the monarchy—and to enlarge the estate that a clique of Junkers and industrialists had presented to him at the expense of some East Prussian peasants.

There is nothing of real interest in this German figure, unless it be Hindenburg's disloyalty. Instead of turning down the offer of the republic he hated, and supporting the royalist activities of his own caste, Hindenburg twice took the oath to the republic's flag only to betray its colors twice. He seems indeed patterned after one of the treacherous heroes of Wagner's *Nibelungen*.

But far from being disgusted, the Germans admired and even loved him—some because the "poor old man" had lost the war, others because he kept on defending his unfortunate emperor, still others out of respect for the "aged man who had swallowed his aristocratic pride" and lent himself to ruling a bourgeois democracy. And many people were simply fond of the fine figure he cut in his bemedaled uniform, with his head "as though carved in wood." Even Americans were taken in by German propaganda, and believed him to be the "faithful stalwart of the German people."

Fond as the average German is of neurasthenic actors, an old man weighing three hundred-odd pounds and therefore evidently good-hearted, naïve, and honest appears to him equally lovable. And how good it was to tell one's children about the struggles the great old man had gone through when he accepted office (and a large country estate into the bargain). It is memorable indeed that in their first free election of a boss—the first in one thousand years—the Germans voted into office a not very bright aged Junker who later was able to pull the wool over their eyes.

Adolf Hitler (1889–?). His success with the Germans is due to two different qualities, both absent in any of his predecessors as Germany's rulers: he was the first "man of the people" to have gained authority since Luther, and he was the first political orator the Germans have ever had. The Kaiser, who has so much in common with Hitler, would only occasionally speak in public, and Bismarck never. The Liberal and Socialist parties had a number of good speakers, but none of them carried the masses with them.

Hitler literally talked his way into power. He never would have succeeded without radio. Methodically he trained both his voice and his gestures, and, with the Wagnerian opera singer always in mind, developed his natural gift as an actor. It is a fact that he directed the men at the searchlights by signs from his platform to support the effect of his worked-up ecstasies, which regularly culminated in thrown-up arms and a breaking of the voice.

Perhaps that ecstasy came partly from sincere emotion—as happens to any actor. Unlike Mussolini, who had but cynical contempt for his people, Hitler may have believed in the superiority of the German nation. The complete ineffectualness of Hitler's speeches in print proves that his effects were based on oratory and *mise en scène*. Bismarck's speeches make good reading—he was a sincere thinker and stylist, and a poor speaker.

Original anecdotes or examples such as enliven the speeches of a Gladstone, a Jefferson, or a Lincoln (in any case indications of true personality) are completely absent in Hitler's speeches. Not a single simile is taken from nature, history, rural life, or the crafts. Endless repetition is the outstanding characteristic of his style.

A continuous alternation between screaming and whining reveals the hysterical daydreams of vengeance and destruction which mark Hitler's personality. One wonders how some people could ever compare a man like Hitler, a leader who destroyed the last vestige of law, with a Napoleon who on the very night preceding his *coup d'état* set up two commissions for the drafting of a new code. Everything in Hitler breathes vengeance for early humiliations. Because he himself came from decidedly mixed stock he turned against mixed races; he hated Austria because his Austrian countrymen seem not to have had much use for him as a youngster; turned down by the Vienna art academy in the early 1900s, he centered his wrath upon the painting style of that epoch; not knowing the art of enjoying life, he loathed the French who know it so well; frustrated in the company of women, he banned them from public life; and since he himself had no learning he set out to persecute all knowledge. He hates mankind, beauty, and nature, and loves only power.

But he gave the Germans more than mere oratory; he also gave them what they had so sorely missed in the colorless days of the late republic—uniforms, flags, high boots, parades, medals, and military music. And above all he re-established authority—which they prefer to responsibility. Here, after long, somber years, was a man after the people's heart: he relieved them from the embarrassment of having to form and voice their own opinions, and did all thinking—and voting—for them, as kings and Junkers had done from time immemorial.

On May 1, 1933, I listened over the radio to Hitler's speech before an audience of many thousands. As he yelled "obedience!" and repeated that word twice, the masses were audibly swept by a real frenzy of enthusiasm. As other nations hail freedom, the Germans hailed obedience; the new leader had found the key to their hearts.

Soon propaganda built around him a growing legend. It was rumored that he accepted no salary as chancellor, living on his royalties only; that he had sacrificed to the fatherland every thought of family life; that he kept his head clear by teetotalism and vegetarianism. After a few months in office, and before he had accomplished a thing, the Germans already looked up to him as if to a saint. But nothing impressed them more than the wholesale killings of June 30, 1934, in which he did away with eleven hundred of his own followers.

What a man! Nobody, of course, minded that he had inherited the treacherous tendencies of many of his precursors. Apart from that, he but little resembled old Hindenburg. These were two thoroughly different men indeed who met when Hitler first faced the aged field marshal: a middle-aged civilian in ill-fitting clothes stood before a powerful figure who for seventy years had been accustomed to wear the tight army uniform; the man with the most elaborate mustache in the country looked at the tiniest mustachio on any German's lip; a healthy, nerveless giant faced a neurasthenic; a hearty eater a vegetarian; a *pater familias* an eternal bachelor. There stood a Protestant Prussian Junker and a renegade Catholic petty bourgeois of Austrian descent. Hindenburg, a product of good breeding, believed firmly in a class society, while Hitler, a product of class society, put all his stock in racial concepts. A rationalist encountered a hazy mystic; a taciturn man whose career had been orderly and systematic was face to face with a talkative upstart.

The Germans loved the new taskmaster's ways: never to work through persuasion, rarely by flattery, but mostly by threats and always with lies. Since Hitler was fundamentally a frightened man, he counted on the fright of others. Although the mere look of his eyes gave the lie to him, the insolent frankness with which he revealed his program long before he assumed office was passed off as "German candor." His perpetual pathological cry for "recognition" was familiar to German ears.

By ridiculing knowledge and scholarship Hitler gave strength to the fatal bias against intellectuals as men of action. And while he thus curried favor with the uneducated, the educated fell prey to his promises of national glory. Hitler's persecution of intellectual values climaxed the age-old German schism of spirit and State.

Not Hitler's cruelty itself, but its "moral justification" fascinated the Germans. Whereas to the American the idea of a "lack of recognition" is absurd, the German, feeling that lack with tremendous emotional force, girds himself to destroy his "envious neighbor." Hitler could not have succeeded without the German's terrible awareness of world-wide contempt for the German nation—fictitious though that contempt may have been. The old conflict between "sense of honor" and arrogance formed the psychological basis of all the horrors through which a jealous people seeks escape.

The more openly Hitler rearmed and the more openly he threatened his hated enemies, the greater his following grew—until finally he gave the Germans their greatest national need: military service The man in the street watched the generals take orders from this common man; he saw university teachers and big business alike support his politics, and gave little thought to the consequences. But he apparently overlooked the fact that armament profits and high wages had something to do, after all, with support from both big business and labor. With such heterogeneous groups as the army and the universities, capital and labor, saying "yes" to the master-race doctrine, its validity and righteousness seemed clear enough. How could Germany's youth be expected to withstand the temptation?

Moreover, the things that Hitler attacked and destroyed were far from being respected by the masses. How many Germans were Christians in their hearts? The persecution of Jews and Communists was entirely in line with their ancient antipathies.

Hitler knew how to fulfill the most fundamental desires by bringing them both uniforms *and* "philosophy," the rattling saber *and* music. He was a harsh taskmaster, but at the same time flattered their lust for vengeance. Rearmament provided work for all; a simple method— its price was merely that liberty which the Germans had tried for fourteen years and had never come to respect. But above all Hitler gave them back their self-confidence—that assurance they claimed they had lost at Versailles in 1919, but which in reality they had never possessed.

Germany had long been accepted as a full member of the League and its Council; she had long taken part in the various international congresses, winning honors at times; her transatlantic shipping held the blue ribbon and her industrialists had their shares in international cartels. But in spite of all this the Germans still felt wronged. Propaganda had hammered home to them that the War Guilt Clause of the Versailles Treaty had dishonored them—and this was where Hitler came in.

In fact, the Versailles Treaty had long been worthless. Its three main provisions—Reparations, Disarmament, and Occupation—had long been discarded. Hitler, who boasted of tearing up the "ignominious treaty," in truth tore up a meaningless sheet of paper—for all practical purposes in 1933 the Treaty no longer existed. But the mere feeling of revolt against "injustice" intoxicated the Germans. The masses did not see through the fraud, and the few who did kept silent.

And so this warrior nation accepted World War II with the same passion and confidence with which it had welcomed the Kaiser's war—as a "people's war." Few realized that the time of world conquest was over, that inevitably the other powers would unite in a feeling of global solidarity to meet the new Teutonic peril. Few stopped to think that their nation, under this new leadership, might lose again.

3 KINGS AND JUNKERS

THE AMERICAN whose ancestors drove George III out of his colonies has a certain weakness for the kings that others have kept on modern thrones as a romantic relic. He cannot get enough of titles, courts, and curtsies on the stage or screen or in newspaper articles. Royalty appears to him as a caged lion: one admires the noble beast as long as there is no danger.

Occasionally an American writer suggests a constitutional monarchy for Germany. He fails to realize that, no matter how many millions of monarchists Germany has, there is no monarch, that is to say, no available talent of royal blood. Out of the hundred and twenty-odd sons and grandsons of the runaway kings and princes of 1918 not a single one has distinguished himself by energy, intelligence, or personal charm. Two or three of them were killed in war. And none of them so much as lifted a finger when their own role of ruler was snatched from them by a mere house painter, who believed, if not in the German people, at least in himself. Not republican sentiments but the lack of an outstanding monarch prevented the Germans from re-establishing the monarchy.

Coming to Germany now as a soldier, the American will probably visit those royal castles that still exist, and perhaps even one of the surviving descendants of the last emperor. He has heard in history classes about the Hohenzollerns. If now near the Berlin *Schloss* h comes across the monuments to the Great Elector and Frederick the Great, he faces two of the three rulers who established both Prussia's power and her ill-famed militarism. For "Prussia" means more than a territory—it means a philosophy, a way of life, a character.

Precisely three hundred years ago a comparatively small German prince who could not even call himself a king built up with daring and an iron fist the first exemplary German army. He began the very year the Thirty Years' War ended—that conflagration which had destroyed Germany, certainly in every military sense. Why did this happen in Prussia, why of all possible places in Berlin and Potsdam?

Prussia is built on sandy ground, which produces chiefly rye and potatoes. The cold uniformity and dullness of her wide plains are broken only occasionally by modest hills, and often darkened by pine woods harboring game.

Berlin became a capital by chance. It was built without any plan, and after a short period of fairly good taste has in the past eighty years grown to be the ugliest capital in the world. Berlin lacks London's greenery, the gorgeous avenues of Paris, the romantic hills of Rome, the grandiose double harbor of New York. The only lung giving breath to its millions is the *Tiergarten,* a public park surrounded by huge city streets and stone buildings without style. The park itself is well organized, clean, and displays not a trace of imagination; it is impossible to get away from the hundreds of verboten signs which hinder free movement; everything is kept within military lines.

As the three great pyramids suddenly and unexpectedly rise from the Egyptian desert, so the Prussian State pyramid has been erected on the sandy plains of Brandenburg. No Rameses or Cheops lies buried there—it is liberty.

It was only possible to fashion that kind of military State from a dull and unrefined people that had no ambition then and has no ideals now, unless the will to power. Originally less German than Germany's south and west, medieval Brandenburg-Prussia got her lifeblood from the Slav east.

Already at that time Prussia had a warrior caste which through robbery and inheritance had come into possession of wide stretches of eastern land where people talked Polish and some Slav dialects. Those "two hundred families" (to use an American term) promised their sovereign to protect him from foreign aggression both east and south if the prince himself would secure their own estates and privileges—the old feudal form of mutual insurance. Thus the energetic elector built up an officers' corps out of his landed Junkers, while the Junkers themselves organized battalions and regiments by pressing their peasants into military service for thirty years. War or no war, these Prussian peasants lived as armed slaves all their lives. For three or four months they were sent home every year to till their own soil and sire new soldiers for their Junkers and princes. Schoolteachers and pastors were mere servants of the Junkers, dependent on their every whim. Moreover, most Junkers also held the office of local judge, and thus were masters over all civic life.

This is how Germany bred her superior army, and soon her brilliant general staff school as well. When kings and Junkers with that army subdued foreign, particularly Eastern, regions, they spoke of carrying German culture to the barbarians. Sword and whip were the paraphernalia of that *Kultur*. The people were kept in bondage by harsh methods and cruel punishment. From military coercion, hate, and subordination the Prussian style was built, and made so secure for three hundred years to come that Prussian rulers had no worries of possible revolt.

"Potsdam is nothing but a huge guardhouse," so Schelling, the great philosopher, said after a visit; "a prison from which there is no way out. All bridges are guarded so as to make it a virtual island. It was here that soldiers kept under constant control were trained to become the heroes of the Seven Years' War. What cruelties were the price of that glory! How much torture, despair, and disaster have those silent stone buildings witnessed!" And Lessing called Prussia a "prison State."

That "prison" was filled by methods similar to those of the slave trade which continued until recent times in Ethiopia and the Sudan. Throngs of foreign subjects were kidnaped or bought by Prussian kings, who later hired them out again as mercenaries for foreign wars such as England's colonial expeditions. The usual price of a soldier was from seven to eight pounds. Besides the King of Prussia it was particularly the dukes of Hesse and Brunswick who bought and sold their subjects like cattle. Once sent abroad, such soldiers were not permitted to return before the war was over. Among civilized nations such methods were unique at a time when the United States and France had long since adopted the Rights of Man. At the time of Washington's presidency Prussia had a "military budget" instead of a constitution. All members of the cabinet were called "war ministers," all tax collectors "war commissars." Up to 1918 many civil servants in Germany wore uniforms.

It is hard for an American to believe that similar conditions, only slightly modified, still prevailed in the domain of the German Junkers of yesterday. True, peasants had obtained the franchise; but woe to any "wrong vote" discovered by the Junker's representative! The unfortunate voter was sure to be found out the next morning and disciplined. In fact, the complete political impotence of the common man was still extant in the province of Brandenburg, and in East Prussia a number of decades after the end of Russian peasant serfdom and the abolition of slavery in this country.

The sons of Prussian Junkers inherited their power; and when Prussia in 1871 was put at the helm of the Reich and the Prussian king became German emperor, the Junkers took over in the whole of Germany. For like their forebears they still got all key positions both in the army and public administration.

They were military experts. Under Frederick the Great they had attained such perfection in the art of warfare that Napoleon himself held them in respect. These Junkers had no love for war as such—they were neither fanatics nor sadists. Warfare simply happened to be

their inherited profession, taken for granted as shipbuilders or musi
cians accept their hereditary métier. Public recognition and profitable
jobs made life easy for them, especially during what they called inter
war periods, that is in the decades of preparation for war. No wonder
they grew to be masters in a craft which secured for them both social
standing and pecuniary reward.

But unfortunately the activities of the Junkers were by no means
limited to the military profession. The sovereigns, who up to 1918
lived in complete segregation from the man in the street, filled all
their ministries and governorships with members of the Junker fami
lies whom they had befriended—even when these professional war
riors had not the slightest training for such jobs. Whereas German
universities formed the center of European learning, and their philoso
phers and scientists attained world fame, the scions of Junker families
limited their education to the general staff academy (*Kriegsschule*)
and an occasional university term, mostly spent in beer drinking and
dueling. Thus the Junker leaders of the State had no real knowledge
of languages or history. Nor did they really know their own people.
If one of them did engage in serious studies or in writing, he was
likely to be called a degenerate and soon also stricken from the wait
ing lists for higher appointments. And this though in London, Vienna
and Paris the most reactionary aristocrats were, and still are, often
men of erudition.

The first president of the United States left thirty-seven volumes of
his own writings. Jefferson, Franklin, Wilson, and others were schol
ars. The French tradition of the *Académie* forms an uninterrupted
line of scholar statesmen from Richelieu to Herriot. Only in Germany
was a man of action who was also a savant looked at askance.

As late as 1909 Junker journals said of Bethmann-Hollweg that he
brought nothing to his newly assumed chancellorship—or did he per
haps fancy that the study of Kant would be of any use at the Wilhelm
strasse? Five years later the same man was called upon to declare war
and "justify" the invasion of Belgium by the typically German prov

erb "Need knows no heed." But when the Kaiser learned that his chancellor held no army reserve commission, he at once ordered a uniform to be made for him overnight (for Bethmann-Hollweg was a very tall man and could not wear ready-made clothes); for it would have been ridiculous to have a gentleman in mufti read the declaration of war before the German Reichstag. Germans are always amused to see pictures of the secretary of war of some foreign country reviewing a regiment in mufti, hat in hand.

Thus Prussia, and later on Germany, was for three hundred years ruled by ignorant and often incompetent noblemen. They knew how to make war, but they knew nothing of politics—and thus these Junkers, winning practically all wars, never did learn how to rule in peacetime. It was a situation unique in history. Every military success merely added to the tenacity with which the victorious Junkers clung to their monopoly of political administration. Their class produced one single statesman of stature: Bismarck—and him they hate.

Austria, always Prussia's antipode, has given birth in her semi-southern landscape, full of fruit and wine, to an amiable Catholic stock which, oriental rather than German, is artistic and utterly non-military in its mode of life. Not by coincidence is Austria the habitat of music. The Hapsburgs did not themselves create that spirit, but they came to symbolize it, and at any rate were wise and experienced enough to win many a peace after a lost war, and to ally themselves by marriage with other European courts. Austria gave Germany a dozen emperors, and although among all the Hapsburgs there were not more than three great rulers—one of them a woman—they preserved their throne longer than any European dynasty. Vienna was founded a thousand years before Berlin.

Nearly all the beautiful domes, castles, monasteries, and town halls the foreigner admires in Germany are to be found in the south and west of the country and in provinces annexed by Prussia.

A warrior nation such as Prussia, that within three centuries was defeated only twice and managed to rise from a margraviate to an empire, must owe its success primarily to its fitness for war. Prussia is the Sparta of German-speaking peoples, as Austria, with her poetry, her music, and architecture, is their Athens. Sparta, too, won wars, and yet her name would long be forgotten were she not put up as an example every few centuries by people such as the Nazis, who also won battles and who will also be obliterated.

The fateful split between spirit and State[1] was not confined to Prussia alone. Compared to what French or English men of letters received from their kings, their German brethren got very little indeed from the courts of Munich, Dresden, and Weimar. Moreover, the influence of these men of letters on public affairs was nil in the German principalities; while it can safely be assumed that Italian or French history would have taken a different course without the influence of Italian or French men of letters.

There are three instances, within three hundred years, of men of letters who tried to rule on German soil. All of them failed. For ten years Goethe spent half of his time attempting to introduce modern government to the little principality of his friend the Duke of Weimar —he withdrew an embittered man. Wilhelm von Humboldt strained all his efforts to make the Prussian government more human and more spiritual-minded—he gave it up after less than a year. And in the infant German republic Walther Rathenau essayed something similar only to be murdered by the Nazis after he had been five months in office.

Certainly there were patrons enough among German princes—men who tried to furnish their lives with arts and sciences. The less political power a principality had, the more likely would one find at its petty court some evidence of erudition and refinement; and this was particularly true of Bavaria and the Rhineland. Austria always led in that respect. But Prussia remained much more crude than her neighbors, both German and non-German.

The good reputation of Frederick the Great—nowhere paralleled—

[1] These problems have been dealt with at length in *The Germans* by the same author

is based on a popular fallacy. His short-lived support of the American fight for independence made him appear to Americans as a friend of liberty; but in fact his real interest was to harm England. He was regarded as a pioneer of intellectual progress, too, because of his conquettish sympathy for Voltaire; but the truth is that as a young man Frederick was no more than an ambitious conqueror who plunged his country without any reason into a war which was to be followed by two others. To his subjects he gave less freedom than even the Roi Soleil. He arranged for the robbing of foreigners in his country when it so pleased him. And in his memoirs he confesses that "if kings rule they do as they like, and leave it to wretched jurists to vindicate their doings thereafter"—a passage which reads like *Mein Kampf*.

Frederick's lack of understanding of what Germans outside of Prussia accomplished in his own day is well shown through his comments on Goethe's work and his contempt for Lessing and Herder. When he summoned Bach and thus came face to face with the one real German genius he was to see in his life, it was merely to show off his own powers as a flutist; he did not give Bach the court position he had hoped for.

What Prussia's spiritual leaders proclaimed later merely seems to repeat Frederick's ideas. Here are some samples out of a hundred and twenty years:

The philosopher Fichte: "There is no law between countries, and no right except the right of the stronger."

The philosopher Hegel: "War is eternal and moral."

The chemist Ostwald, Nobel prize (1894): "I cannot acknowledge any source of Right except Force."

The historian Treitschke (1896): "Whoever preaches the nonsense about perennial peace has not the slightest concept of national life. Our army is a glorious form of German idealism."

General Bernhardi, classical militarist: "President Taft's suggestion of a court of arbitration between great powers must be discredited. War must be given back its moral justification. War calls forth the highest powers of human nature. Individual atrocities fade before the idealism of the whole enterprise."

Thomas Mann in 1914: "Our soldiering spirit is related to our morality. Whereas other cultures, even in their art, tend toward a civilian pattern of ethics, German militarism remains a matter of German morals. The German soul is too deep to find civilization its highest conception. . . . Germany's full virtue and beauty unfold only in wartime. . . .

Adolf Hitler: "Humaneness is but a mixture of stupidity and cowardice."

There is no place for Prussia in the German Hall of Fame; not a single universally known thinker or writer came from Prussia. Where did the great Germans hail from? There is Gutenberg from Mayence; Kepler and Grünewald from Swabia; Dürer, Cranach, and Holbein from Bavaria and Franconia; Luther from Saxony. Then in the innermost sanctum of the temple: Goethe and Schiller and Hölderlin; Bach, Gluck and Haydn, Mozart and Schubert. They were followed by others: Weber, Schumann and Wagner, Johann Strauss, Brahms and Bruckner, Jean Paul and Novalis, Leibnitz and Schopenhauer, Hegel and Schelling, Liebig and Bunsen, down to the *dii minores gentium* of our own days, such as Zeppelin or Richard Strauss—South German all of them, Saxons, Austrians, or citizens of the Free Hanseatic cities.

Here are more great Germans who have nothing to do with Prussia: Beethoven, half Rhenish, half Fleming; Kant, who was of Scotch-Franconian ancestry; the Humboldts, descended from semi-French Huguenots; Nietzsche, who called himself a Pole. To them must be added a number of pure-blooded Jews to whose fame Germany may no longer lay claim: Mendelssohn, Meyerbeer, Offenbach, Marx, Heine. Klopstock fled Prussia and went to Denmark, as Herder escaped to Riga and Winckelmann to Rome. The one Prussian of stature is Heinrich von Kleist, who wrote, incidentally, that his country must have been laid bare by the retreating ocean through some error of nature.

On one of the great squares of Berlin the American will find a huge building and a smallish red brick house. The great building is the Reichstag. For the inscription on its frieze—"To the German People" —the German people itself had to wait until the time of World War I. The house, partially screened, is the home of the Prussian general staff. Passers-by lower their voices in front of it as if it were haunted. From it has emanated at least once in every generation that fateful sheet of paper, the Order of Mobilization, signed by the king or emperor without consultation with the Reichstag across the square. And each time the nation has accepted that paper with enthusiasm; later on to countersign it in blood.

If no gracious bomb has done away with it, the American will find in the Berlin Tiergarten arrayed in two straight rows of marble statues all the twenty rulers of the house of Hohenzollern. Their characteristic on-parade array shows them as Prussian kings. Among them there were three outstanding men; the rest counted for little or nothing at all. It is curious that almost regularly a spendthrift followed a thrifty king; William II was the last spendthrift. Behind each of those crowned army officers who look down with the searching eye of the born leader at the commoner below there are two small busts of contemporaries—generals, cabinet ministers, and now and then a civilian. Among the latter are Handel and Kant—collateral figures, so to speak. The kings in whose giant shadows they stand have long been forgotten outside Germany; yet these collateral figures have carried German fame into the world.

That marble array is a symbol of the German tragedy. The spirit never attained power in Germany, while the men in power had no part in intellectual life themselves. For four centuries, from Luther and Kepler to Diesel and Einstein, the German spirit sat at home like Cinderella, while power problems were solved outside. Kings and

Junkers, who determined the fate of the German nation, fought their battles without ideals, and won their victories against the spirit of their age.

The American who comes to Germany is likely to descend from a line of men who for one hundred and seventy years have chosen their administrators by free vote. He knows, as did his ancestors, that he can attain any office for which he qualifies. What special privileges he may have seen working at home and what injustice he has experienced have been exceptions.

The Germans, whom he now finds in utter chaos, are the descendants of men who began to vote a hundred years after Americans. Up to 1918 the franchise in provincial elections still depended on the voter's financial status. Popular influence in vital debate on the floor of the Reichstag was always negligible; the right to declare war was the Kaiser's, who in 1914 was in a position to sign declarations of war according to his own judgment or caprice. No one could contest his decision; in that respect he could claim almost papal infallibility. Even if the nation through its representatives had actually voted against war appropriations, war would have been waged nonetheless—as it was by the Prussia of 1866.

But the German man in the street can be relied on to give his consent to war. In fact, the German masses have at all times flocked to the warring armies. They are happy if they can take orders from men who by birth are near the top of the pyramid. Here are three examples taken from the history of the past hundred years:

(1) In 1848 a few hundred German representatives assembled in Frankfurt—sent there not by general elections, to be sure, but yet in accordance with public opinion. Their task was to prepare for a unified liberal Germany. There were many high-minded, farsighted men among them, thinkers and men of action, and they had come with the best of intentions. And whom did they choose as their head? A little Austrian archduke. They could not conceive of their *Reichsverweser* (Protector of the Realm) without a princely title and uniform.

(2) In 1867 Bismarck called the first assembly of the North German League. In drafting the constitution the question arose whether the federated countries should follow the English pattern of a constitutional monarchy or remain under the supreme will of their royal rulers—in short, whether cabinet ministers should be responsible to the people or to the king. Eighty per cent of the votes were cast for the latter solution—the assembly virtually voted itself out of existence. And this was the first meeting of German representatives assembled by free election.

(3) When the German people for the first time in a thousand years were called upon in 1925 to elect their own chief executive, they did not choose a democratic civilian, some vigorous man with real strength of mind—no, they chose Von Hindenburg, the octogenarian Junker field marshal of the runaway Kaiser, who in his whole life had done no more than lose a war.

These were the great free decisions the German nation made in the past hundred years. All three were bows to military power, to kings and Junkers. All three were voluntary renunciations of liberty—a threefold treason of the German spirit.

4   IMPOTENCE OF THE SPIRIT

WHEN HITLER ROSE to power nothing baffled the outside world so much as the jubilation of four or five thousand German university professors over this dawn of a new epoch of force and lawlessness. In 1914, ninety-three outstanding German intellectuals had in a pronunciamento approved and hailed the invasion of Belgium; in 1933 no less than twelve hundred German professors hailed the dawn of Hitlerian barbarism. Loudest among them were the psychiatrists. What would American psychiatrists do if an American Hitler tried to gain prominence? They would probably set up a commission to examine his mental condition. Their German colleagues acted differently in 1933. Nine of them, all men of great repute, at once formed a "preliminary" committee, and published a declaration (with a preface by the Swiss psychoanalyst Jung) urging all members of the *Allgemeine Gesellschaft für Psychiatrie* (General Society of Psychiatry) to study Hitler's *Mein Kampf.* "We presume," they said, "that our members have studied Hitler's book with full scholarly earnestness, and accept it as fundamental."

The fact that the first scientific circle to applaud Hitler originated among psychiatrists is not only material for a comedy but also a monument to the cowardice of German professors. I personally know of only two instances of voluntary resignation on the part of university teachers: the Berlin theologian Barth, a Swiss, and the archaeologist Curtius in Rome. Of course there may be more.

The responsibility of the German universities, and with it their guilt, matches that of the Junkers. The German university teacher enjoyed far greater esteem than his American colleague, because he was always an original scholar and had gained his position on the strength of his own research work. Up to 1920 the popular admiration for science as such was greater in Germany than in any other country. Old Heidelberg has its intellectual and spiritual traditions as the Lutheran Church has hers. And since the Germans knew that these powers were loyal to the sovereign and never in the opposition, they conceded them an influence on educational matters.

Whenever it came to the point of protecting the spirit and intellectual progress, the German professors, including theologians, as a rule shrank from the issue. The enthusiasm of some university students for the Polish and Greek fight for liberation in the thirties of the past century was hastily quelled by their teachers, lest the movement grow to a desire for German liberties. When Berlin University once celebrated old Goethe's birthday, a royal rescript came down, warning the students against too much zeal. Members of fraternities which had dared to follow the French custom of erecting "trees of liberty" were denied the necessary licenses to establish themselves as doctors or lawyers; thirty-nine of them were condemned to death, though the penalties were later commuted to long prison terms. But of the universities not one had lifted a finger in their defense. Three or four professors occasionally "recommended" a constitution for Germany in those days, defying the danger of imprisonment. All that happened roughly a hundred years prior to Nazism.

The refusal of seven Göttingen professors to transfer their oath of allegiance from one sovereign to another (who, incidentally, was a nincompoop) was a unique case in German history, and became famous as such. They were promptly dismissed because "criticism of the sovereign's decisions by citizens with the limited powers of mind at a subject's disposal cannot be tolerated." This happened in 1837— at a time, that is, when other nations, not superior in intelligence to Germans, had long had their own constitutions.

Some years after that the King of Prussia opened his first parliament in similar tones. "Petitions may be submitted," he said, "but no opinions voiced." According to Humboldt, a Hanoverian king once said that "professors, whores, and dancing girls can all be bought for money; they'll go everywhere they are offered a few pennies more."

With all that degradation of the spirit, book sales in Germany increased whenever the power of the State diminished; they decreased when that power again gained strength. In 1805, under Napoleonic oppression, 4,000 German books were printed; in 1812, the year preceding the liberation of the principalities, only 2,000. At a time of complete national disunity, in 1843, 14,000 volumes were published; in 1872, after the great victory over France, not more than 11,000.

But even so, these figures go way beyond the figures of book production in other countries. This, and the output of writers and composers, is the glory that is Germany. In the days of humiliation of German genius, Germany, according to the French historian Taine, was "for fifty years the source of all contemporary ideas. No other nation," he said, "has ever possessed a better faculty for discovering general ideas than the Germans of those days." The French never forgot the intellectual merits of their enemy. On Beethoven's one hundredth birthday, in December 1870, while the Germans were besieging Paris, the Parisians had the brilliant idea of christening one of the guns defending their capital: Beethoven.

As savants, artists, too, were trodden underfoot by princes and Junkers. Within one single century the German genius produced seven composers unmatched by any other nation: Bach discovered eternity in music, Handel the world's brilliance, Haydn nature, Gluck heroism, Mozart the heavens, Beethoven sorrow and victory, and Schubert the singing human heart. They follow each other closely, as though each had passed on a ring of mastership to the other.

All of them were sons of the people, offspring of blacksmiths, game wardens, lackeys, or cooks. In order to succeed they had either to accept humiliations at home or to go abroad. In Vienna a number of wealthy aristocrats gave financial support to composers—to secure for themselves, through the masters' dedications, a share in their immortality. But shameful degradation at the hand of their sovereigns left its mark in the hearts of the masters. Bach was jailed because of "disobedience"; Mozart was forced to eat with the servants and once was struck in the face by a count; Haydn had to fight stubbornly to be properly addressed by his bread giver. Only Beethoven asked for equality and due honor.

The greatest virtuosos, as a rule, were allowed to play before German princelings only during meals. A duke of Baden was fond of having his orchestra so placed that he could aim and spit at the bald head of the drummer.

When once in a while a great man did speak up at a German university, he was either bitterly denounced or dismissed. Such things happened throughout four centuries, from Kepler to Einstein. Thus the German people in great crises were left without the support of their potential spiritual leaders, and piously followed the Junker war lords like cattle. The Germans believed in the wisdom of their rulers because they saw their decisions backed by German intellectual leadership. As other peoples need the priest's blessing before they set out for an adventure, the Germans find their peace of mind by listening to a philosophical justification of their own bellicose nature. German guns contain, as it were, besides 95 per cent metal, an alloy of 5 per cent philosophy—a philosophy, that is, which gives the German a feeling of righteousness in his conquests.

If in the decisive moments of 1866, 1914, 1933, and 1939 leaders of the German intelligentsia had risen as one man in a grandiose protest, surely at least a part of the population would have felt embarrassed to join in the outrages of their rulers. But German professors did exactly the opposite. The decent minority found itself overpowered by the loudmouthed advice of the "spiritual leaders."

The first to accept that submission of spirit to State was one of the rare upright Germans—Martin Luther. True, he was a popular hero—but for a single hour only. It was a supreme moment in a German's life when he stood, a little runaway monk with no family to back him, by himself before the emperor and the papal nuncio in Worms, and dared to oppose the two greatest powers of his time. That hour, unique in their history, should have taught the Germans what courage means in the face of princes and priests; among other nations such episodes grew to be examples for generations to come!

But perhaps Martin Luther's great hour was born in ecstasy. In fact, the rest of his life, before and after that hour, was filled with weakness and doubt. As a student he was emotionally unstable, afraid of his own senses; he fled into the fold of monastic life, broke out, and got married. He recanted half of what he said and did, only to repent his own recantations. When the German peasants rose and turned to his spiritual revolt for support, Luther in deep alarm withdrew from them, and thus through the weight of his name broke the backbone of that first German revolution.

He was born a proletarian, and remained completely independent of the lure of money and pleasure, living as a modest divine without any mundane ambition. Of his own will he turned over to the princes the power he had wrested from the Pope, and proclaimed them as masters over the faith of their subjects. The man who had not yielded to the highest spiritual power on earth gave way to the worldly power. Said he, "War service and the sword, in spite of their horrible consequences, must be faced with manly eyes; war is divine service, and as necessary to the world as eating and drinking." So afraid was Luther of princes that he, although secretly only, sanctioned the bigamy of the Landgrave of Hesse—an offense the landgrave himself used to punish with death.

Like other Germans, Luther dreaded and revered State power. He grew deeply alarmed when his own spiritual problems seemed to change into issues of domestic power politics. The German intellectual has courage so long as he deals with invisible antagonists; the moment an armed adversary, a visible police officer, turns up, he gives way to the uniform. For he himself wears only civilian garb, be it the monk's cowl or the burgher's coat. The barricade-storming intellectual revolutionary is unknown in German history. Order is always preferable to revolution in Germany, and obedience is better than liberty.

Luther, who had so grandiose a beginning, was fundamentally a poet rather than a revolutionary. Since in action Germans could only take orders, they attained genuine greatness as thinkers and poetical dreamers. Thus it was as a musician and a creative linguist that Martin Luther, too, found refuge from the world—a true German, he was frightened of what he had himself unleashed.

For four hundred years the Germans have referred to that example of human weakness whenever there has been question of defying authority. According to Luther, revolution was not permitted—and the Germans believed this.

The second to give in was Kant. He carried a whole universe in his head, and knew how to form it anew. And yet he was threatened with dismissal by one of the most thick-headed Prussian kings for expounding his deist beliefs in the classroom. And what did the great Kant do? Did he live up to the examples of antiquity, and, like Socrates, defend what he held to be true? By no means. As a good German he chose a careful middle course, gave in, and at the same time drafted a paper in his own defense which, locked up in his desk, was found only after his death by his disciples.

In such drawers the great German thinkers have always kept their opinions on the barbarism of the higher-ups, or they have given vent to their judgment in intimate letters or posthumously published memoirs. In every country the best minds are always critical; only blockheads agree with everything done in their family or their country. What has not Dante said about Italy, Voltaire about France, or Carlyle about England!

But nowhere was the criticism on the part of outstanding thinkers as annihilating, resentment as deep-rooted as in Germany—because open discussion was always *verboten* and revolt always unimaginable.

The following opinions on Germany are culled from German thinkers who outwardly never attacked their government. They belong to those voices of underground history without which factual history would be incomplete.

Luther: "There is no salvation for a people where everyone follows his own purpose. That barbarian and really bestial nation! Those ghastly swine, half devil, half human!"

Goethe: "Comparing the German people with other nations arouses painful feelings in us, which I try to overcome in every possible way. . . . But that solace is only meager, failing to take the place of the proud awareness of belonging to a great . . . nation.

"The Germans accept nothing they are given; if one hands them the knife by its handle, they say it isn't sharp; if they are handed the blade, they cry out because they are hurt. . . . From times immemorial the Germans have had a way of knowing everything better than the one whose trade it is; they know it better than a man who has spent his life on a thing. . . . To grasp the full scope of German dishonesty one must familiarize himself with German literature.

"Even if Germany ran as far as Rome, she could not run away from herself. Germans are always accompanied by their fatuity, as Englishmen are by their teakettle. . . . These Northerners go to Italy, and all they succeed in is to put their bear on his hind legs, thinking they succeed in teaching him how to dance."

Schiller: "The German Reich and the German nation are two different things. German majesty never rested upon the heads of German princes. The Germans have cultivated their own values, aloof from politics; for even if the Reich went to pieces, German dignity would survive."

Hölderlin (one of the greatest German poets): "I cannot conceive of a people torn asunder more than the Germans. They are craftsmen, thinkers, priests—but not men. They are masters and servants, but never men. . . . Your Germans cling to the necessary; this is why they are so heavy and so little free. Yet all this might be overlooked if they did not lack all feeling for good life, and if the curse of that Godforsaken unnaturalness were not upon them."

Alexander von Humboldt: "In the great world of the French one is free of the petty bourgeois life which prevails in Berlin and Potsdam. . . . The frame of mind of people there is worse than the desert, worse than the ever-gray sky!"

E. M. Arndt (the spiritual leader of the German liberation from Napoleon): "Germans, particularly the wealthy ones, want to be commended and praised, and that by every doorman and lackey. . . . Compare a German fencer with a French one: the former stands on his feet like an ox, and fights like one too; the Frenchman plays about and dances so one would think he holds a straw in his hand, and yet he hits his mark."

Bismarck: "The Germans? They all are petty and narrow-minded. No one works for the common good. Every single one stuffs his own party mattress. Among ourselves we have always been insupportable. It drives away my sleep to think they were destroying again the building I have built up and molded."

Friedrich Hebbel (the greatest German dramatist besides Schiller): "The Germans know beasts of prey to be free. Therefore they are afraid that freedom might change them to beasts themselves. Even if a revolution should spring up someday, the Germans would rather fight for freedom from taxation than for freedom of thought."

Nietzsche: "If I try to imagine the kind of human being that runs contrary to all my instincts, I cannot but think of a German. I cannot stand that race. To mix with them is to be in bad company. They have no sense of nuances. . . . I feel as though the Black Continent where the slaves are still not freed lay near northern Germany. Definition of the Teuton: obedience and long legs. . . . I confess they are my enemies, those Germans. In them I find and despise every possible form of foul ideas and of cowardice in facing an issue. For a thousand years they have managed to mess up practically everything they laid hands on."

The world is still aghast, and at a loss to understand that the nation which has given birth to so much great music and writing and has so distinguished itself in science, in practically every generation falls back again into barbarism. Still the simple fact is not realized that for centuries power and culture have been separated in Germany, allotted to two different classes. The submission of the spirit to the sword accounts also for this last and most terrible of Teutonic outbreaks; but the same phenomenon also determines the guilt.

The most remarkable thing is that the leading German intellectuals themselves have never tried to gain any influence over the government. They seem to be quite happy on their dream island, and only wave when the ship of State sails by; actually they enjoy not having to board it.

Universities failed in their historic role as mediators between power and spirit—if for no other reason, because of their financial dependency on the sovereign. Municipal universities did not exist until recently; private foundations on the American pattern are still unknown. This is why the standards of natural science were ever so much higher than the accomplishments of philosophy, theology, and history—which were all hampered in their development through continuous government supervision. Science did not interfere with public affairs and was let alone. Thus the Germans have had a fair number of good historians of foreign history, but hardly a historian of German history itself that the outside world accepts as an authority. Lamprecht, the leading history teacher, in 1912 praised German world domination as the goal of foreign politics, and called the Kaiser a great ruler.

The most outstanding German scholars have on their visiting cards below their names, "Lieutenant, D.R." (Reserve Lieutenant). On the King's birthday these great men were happy to squeeze their well-developed paunches into their old army tunics, and, lavishly bemedaled, to appear at the governor's reception. A boy's birth was announced in the local paper, "My dear wife has given birth to a new soldier for the Emperor."

One who has watched all this himself in his youth, as has the author, the son of a German professor, and has compared these phenomena with other nations' ways of life, was not astonished when the German spirit resigned itself to Herr Hitler.

5   JEWS AND GERMANS

THE UNDOING of the German Jews was, strangely enough, their very patriotism—their love of Germany. That love accounts for both their influence on matters German and for their downfall. They tried to assimilate themselves in other countries too—and who can blame them for that? Is not the United States built by children of many different peoples, transformed into Americans? But whereas in America a score of different races accommodated themselves to one another on an equal footing, in Europe the Jews always appeared as aliens, often as refugees from other countries, who had to adapt their own ways to the long-settled life habits of an already homogeneous native population.

Thus the Jews, as good citizens, became Englishmen, Russians, or Spaniards; and in accepting the country's customs they gradually took on even the semblance of its original citizens.

Their earliest appearance in northern Europe was evidently in Germany. As early as the eighth century Charlemagne dispatched a number of Jews as envoys to the Near East. But the first documents mentioning Rhineland Jews date from Roman times, and others cover an uninterrupted stretch of a thousand years.

Perhaps the Jews felt at home among Germans because they had certain characteristics in common with them. Their curiosity about foreign lands as well as their gift for acclimatization is not unlike certain German traits. Moreover, they combine imagination with tenacity, commercial efficiency with musical talent. But Germans and Jews are forever set apart from each other by the Jews' love of peace and hatred of war.

When in the eleventh century a German princeling sent out a Jewish merchant to bring him silver swords from Byzantium or rare pelts from the Caucasus which required both daring and wit on the traveler's part, he could count on getting a fund of wonderous tales with these precious wares, as the merchant, displaying some exquisite piece of silk before the princess, related his adventures.

Of a sudden, about the year 1100, the first Jewish persecutions began. They have lasted till this day, and will never cease. Why has Jew-baiting been constantly present in Germany only?

In England the Jews were expelled in a body around 1300—apparently to the last man. For three hundred years there was no object for persecution. Then the Puritans came to the fore; imbued with both their own ardent faith in the Messiah and the legends of the Old Testament, they felt a certain admiration for the "remnants of Israel," and began to grant them all kind of honors, thus avowedly repenting the policies of their forefathers. It is something of a symbol that this only explicit invitation the Jews were ever to receive from a country was based on spiritual considerations.

In Germany no *ex officio* wholesale expulsion was decreed for well over a thousand years, but hundreds of isolated cases of persecutions occurred. With the rise of the German cities, the burgher discovered his own commercial talents, and naturally turned against those who had practically monopolized trade. And what does a businessman do to get rid of a competitor? He calls him an alien. At the same time the Crusades furnished a good excuse. "Fighting the enemy of Christendom begins at home!" became the slogan of those who coveted the businesses and the houses of wealthy Jews; eight hundred years later the "Jewish stab in the back" offered a similar "justification." The Church remained aloof from all this.

Later on it was usury. Moneylending was forbidden to Christians; and the Jews, outside of canon law, were actually forced into that occupation, since they were excluded both from owning land and from the guilds. Their usual rate of interest, 50 per cent, merely followed the pattern set by Roman bankers of old, of whom the "noble murderer Brutus," incidentally, was one of the shrewdest; and the risk of medieval Jews was much greater: once the debtor had asked for his bishop's protection the Jewish moneylenders could no longer sue for their money.

What did the German burgher do when he owed money to a Jew? He burned his house, and with it his own I.O.U.'s. Soon the Jews, frightened by such practices, left rural neighborhoods for the cities and began to lend money on mortgages.

A certain contact between Jews of all countries facilitated the establishment of banking firms. A number of families thus acquired actual wealth; at times kings and ruling princes were among their debtors. When these debts became pressing, they resorted to the old methods. Once an emperor "allowed" the sacking of all Jews in Bohemia and Bavaria—the city of Nuremberg is said to have made two million gold marks on that "permit."

Charles IV felt his peace of mind disturbed by the presence of the Jews in his realm. He was a pallid misanthrope who, like Hitler, sought vengeance for his joyless childhood and the early repression he had suffered. He gave free hand to the mob in Jewish matters. They burned hundreds of them at the stake in Speyer, thousands in Vienna. Some towns in the Rhineland, particularly involved in debts, formed a ring; they drove a few hundred Jews onto a small river island, locked them up in a blockhouse, and burned them alive. (Today they do the same with poison gas.) The fine house of a Strasbourg Jew was subsequently presented by the Emperor to his lady love.

Chronicles which report these atrocities mention no single instance of a burgher raising his voice against the horrors, or trying to protect a Jew. An old Alsatian annalist sums up the Jewish fate by saying that "their own talent is the poison which dooms them." The remark still holds true.

But differences of national characteristics account for different methods employed. Even an anti-Semitic Britisher sticks to the British concept of fair play, and refrains from attacking the weaker fellow when he happens to be his competitor. The ratio of Jews was about the same in Berlin and London (3 per cent); and so was the number of wealthy Jews in both countries. But one cannot imagine a British government engaging in Jew-baiting. Even if some crackpot on the government bench had voiced such ideas, public opinion would not have approved. But unlike the British Government, which depends on public opinion, the German Government has always been free to do as it wished, because there is no such thing as public opinion in Germany.

The Anglo-Saxon in his self-confidence is prepared to acknowledge the merits of a law-abiding alien. The German, lacking any such balance of mind, cannot stand an alien who distinguishes himself. Under constant orders as he is himself, he is prone to take his revenge on the underdog; of all foreigners he likes only spendthrifts. Perhaps the Germans would never have granted civil liberty to their Jews had it not been for Napoleon; or at any rate German Jews would have had to wait about as long as their Russian coreligionists.

During the last century, when no Jew could become an army colonel or governor in Germany—exceptions are negligible—an English Jew was made prime minister, another viceroy of India. Whereas the King of England receives Jewish and Christian church dignitaries alike, the King of Prussia as late as 1900 dispatched a mere police officer to the inauguration of every new Berlin synagogue. While in England a Jew elevated to the peerage takes his oath in the Hebrew language in the House of Lords, German princes and counts are still fond of joking about Jewish customs, and as long as they were in power, forced almost every Jew who aspired to a university or government career to be baptized. My father, who had an international reputation, could not hope for an official career because he refused to be baptized.

Up to 1933 German law made no anti-Jewish discrimination—and accordingly there were no exemptions from military service. Jews were allowed to die for the fatherland, but not allowed to share the social rights of their Gentile fellow citizens. Only a fraction of German Jews answered to such ignominy with disdain; another part did everything in their power to gain "acceptance." This behavior had complex reasons: ambition of a long-oppressed people, genuine patriotism, innate Jewish conservativism—all traits no one can find fault with. And yet that attitude added to the contempt most Germans harbor for Jews. For the average German is not generous but jealous, and therefore tends to take loyalty for weakness; he will soon take advantage of any forbearance shown to him. Nothing short of gruffness impresses him. Germans were suspicious of those Jews who for entirely honorable motives wanted to serve the country beyond what the country allowed them as Jews.

The ultimate cause, however, for the German suspicion was a feeling that the Jew was more adroit and more versatile than the German, and thus his superior in the very accomplishments he craved most himself. Yet he continued to regard him as his inferior in all physical accomplishment—particularly in soldiering.

The most outstanding men in German history have in the main been in favor of the Jews, or at any rate far from anti-Semitic. Luther spoke of them often with enthusiasm; only in his old age, changing many of his opinions, he changed this one too. Goethe compared the Jews to the Germans, and, realizing certain similarities, said, "The Germans should be scattered over the earth like the Jews, to bring to other nations what good there is among them." In both Germans and Jews he denied a talent for commonwealth formation. Humboldt said that he had received his real spiritual education in the Jewish circles of Berlin.

Bismarck as a young representative to the Prussian diet once objected to Jews holding public office; considering popular anti-Jewish feelings in Germany at that time he was quite right. During his thirty years in office he never practiced anti-Semitic politics; once he made a Jew a cabinet minister, a forebear of the author. For five years a Jew was his personal physician, and another was his banker all his life. He once said he would like to see "the German stallion mate with the Jewish mare," and indeed forced his son into a marriage with a titled woman who was the granddaughter of an American Jew. Such was the attitude toward Jews on the part of really great Germans. What now about the outstanding German Jews themselves and their attitude toward Germany?

Jews succeeded most easily as musicians; in fact, musical talent was the only gift the Germans found "pardonable" in them—on that score pre-Hitler Germans were incorruptible. Meyerbeer and Offenbach were among the most popular composers in Germany. Mendelssohn's popularity matches Schumann's. He represents the most interesting case of a German-Jewish crossbreed. At the time when Mendelssohn as a seventeen-year-old lad wrote his *Midsummer Night's Dream* music in Berlin, Weber in London was putting finishing touches to his *Oberon*. Both pieces are imbued with the same aura of air and water and fairyland.

Around 1850, Heine, Marx, and Lassalle, all three representing German-Jewish spirit, were (besides Bismarck and Schopenhauer) the cleverest Germans. All three came from bourgeois stock. All three had embraced the Christian faith at an early age. All three began their careers as philosophers and radical writers. (Outstanding Jewish intellectuals are in general Leftists in politics—contrary to non-political Jewish scholars and businessmen, who usually support the conservative forces of the State.)

Heine spoke with such deeply German accents as a poet that some of his poems became more popular than the verses of Goethe or Schiller. In a Nazi edition of folk poetry his "Lorelei" is given as coming from an "unknown author"; for to exclude those stanzas was impossible. Lassalle, the first leader of German socialism, was passionately national—hence his contacts with Bismarck. Even Marx has his cultural roots in German soil.

All three of these Jewish-born men were attracted to German Gentile women: Marx throughout his life was deeply devoted to his wife, a German baroness; Lassalle loved twice in his short life, both times German aristocrats; and except in his earliest youth, Heine was always in love with some Gentile girl. At the same time the two most prominent Jewesses of Berlin married Gentiles. All this furnishes more proof of a peculiar mutual German-Jewish attraction.

Marx was legally banned from his native country; Lassalle was sent to jail for political reasons; and Heine lived as a self-exile. Yet the critical judgments on German affairs in their writings are not so severe as those mentioned above, coming from Gentile Germans.

A definite preoccupation with "honor" is noticeable in all three of these men. Was that curious oversensitiveness German or Jewish? Were they driven by German mysticism on the Jewish prophetic mission? At any rate all three of them were also driven by dreams of glory; Lassalle promised his beloved he would ride with her in a carriage with four horses through the Brandenburger Tor of Berlin—as the first president of the German republic.

The great internationalist Marx said of Bakunin that the Slavs were culturally inferior to the Germans, and should be educated by them. Heine's nostalgia for Germany grew to be something of a comitragedy, for though he wept for his far-off Germany, in fact he really preferred the life in Paris.

In the new Reich Jews remained practically excluded from public life. During the preparations for World War I and the war itself there was not a single Jew occupying a prominent post in either the government or the general staff. And though there were Jews enough in the Leftist parties, they were not controlled by them. Neither was the German money market under the Jewish thumb, in spite of many wealthy and outstanding Jewish bankers; big business (Krupp, Kirdorf, Thyssen, Stinnes, Vögeler) was Christian.

But in many provinces of German intellectual life the proportion of leading men who were Jews went far beyond their ratio in population figures. Since they were neither preferred by the government nor by public opinion (to say the least) such figures speak for themselves. One per cent was the population ratio of Jews in Germany—yet of the Nobel prizes which went to German citizens 18 per cent went to Jews. Though admitted only to the fringes of university life, their number in higher education was equally out of proportion to that one per cent. Abroad, where people did not discriminate, a surprising number of Jews were among the German citizens who received calls to universities.

On the other hand, the number of Jewish revolutionary leaders is negligible. The revolutionary inclination of Jews is a myth. If nothing else, their eternal role as wanderers has always led them to sympathize with the government that gave them protection. For a thousand years the budgets of many a European ruler were balanced by Jewish money—while the chests of revolutionary factions had surely never any support from Jewish capital. The two head men of the Russian Revolution were non-Jews. Aside from Gambetta in the Paris of 1871, Trotsky is the only leading Jewish figure in the long series of European revolutions. Marx is a good example of the predominantly spiritual part Jews had in revolutionary movement: they are prophets rather than fighters.

Of the twenty-odd leaders of the German revolution of 1918 three were of Jewish extraction. In the fourteen years of the Weimar republic not more than twenty-one Jews held a minister's portfolio out of the two hundred and thirty-odd cabinet ministers who held office during that time in the Reich and the provinces (*Länder*).

But nothing is more significant for German Jewry than the reaction of one of the most powerful German Jews on the collapse of 1918. Ballin, the founder of the HAPAG, committed suicide on the very day his Kaiser, Germany's heir and the war's chief instigator, fled to Holland.

The only Jew ever to be at the head of a German government, Walther Rathenau, was at the same time the only statesman of stature the Weimar republic brought to the fore. As Goethe and Humboldt before him, Rathenau tried to rule in Germany with an eye to spiritual values—and therefore was bound to lose out. As a philosopher and an industrialist he knew his Germans—he did not fool himself as to the risks when he took over.

Limitless love for Germany moved him to take over the government under highly critical conditions. He felt he could serve the country better than others. His passion for the Prussian way of life went so far as to make him buy an old royal mansion; once he toyed with the idea of marrying a Prussian countess.

He was one of the two Jews who saved Germany from defeat in the first two years of the war. On its very first day he realized how short Germany was of essential raw materials, and overnight improvised a government agency to meet that shortage. The other Jew was Haber, the inventor of poison gas, who struggled long with his conscience before he allowed his patriotism to get the better of his humanitarian scruples in releasing the deadly weapon which was his secret.

Rathenau was the first German statesman to win an ally for the isolated German republic by the Russian pact of 1922. And the German people—the people as such—hated him. They did not hate the man Rathenau, whom no one knew and who very seldom appeared before the Reichstag—they hated the idea of a Jew leading Germany. That a Jew should have brought them the country's first success in foreign politics after the defeat—this was an intolerable thought. On his return from Genoa he met with bullets instead of flowers.

His death seemed to relieve the Germans of a burden. I wonder whether any of his liberal colleagues really mourned him. A famous physicist and university teacher refused to cancel his lecture on the day of the chancellor's funeral. But the tomb of Rathenau's murderers was later on made into a "Temple of Heroes" by the Nazis.

Under Nazi rule anti-Semitism reached the climax of two thousand years of Jewish sufferings. What the Spaniards did to them is as nothing compared with Hitler's atrocities; beside him Torquemada appears a ministering angel.

In fact, contemporary German Jew-baiting holds a unique place among all pogroms. In Russia and Romania certain armed groups, with the connivance of the government, attacked Jewish individuals because of their faith; often baptism saved the individual. The civic equality Jews had gained in most countries in the nineteenth century was contested without government interference. That civic equality, however, had been introduced as a matter of administrative expediency, to protect the citizen who happened to be Jewish, not the Jewish community as such. "As a nation we deny them all, but we grant them all as citizens," was said on December 17, 1789, in the Paris Assembly in the motion for Jewish emancipation.

What Hitler did was more than to abolish the civic equality of Jews; he labeled the Jews as a malignant group in the national body which was to be annihilated. The notorious Nuremberg laws and what followed were officially "justified" by the attitude of the Jews themselves, "pernicious to the State." And as the State thus withdrew its protection from the Jews, persecuted them officially, and had them robbed and killed by the mob, the new German law established the principle that a minority actually may be destroyed.

Hitler needed ten years to put that principle into practice. The indignation of the outside world cautioned the German Government to proceed gradually—as it did from the boycott days of 1933 to the wholesale gas killings of 1942. The concepts of "non-Aryanism" and the *numerus clausus* were slowly followed by an application of the so-called non-Aryan principle to special occupational groups, the introduction of the crime of race pollution, et cetera—so that in July 1939 there still lived in Germany 215,000 Jews of her original 560,000.

Hitler's persecution of the Jews had two reasons. Personally, he wanted to take vengeance for the experience in his youth when he had looked for and been given shelter in the Vienna poorhouses supported by Baron Königswarter, a Jew. In these flophouses he had had to live and eat with poor and often ragged Jews, and came to hate them physically. But he also felt a certain superiority in them, and went so far as to say later that the only two vigorous races left were the Germans and the Jews—reason enough to destroy the Jews.

Moreover, before full rearmament the Jews were the only possible subject of attack. They combined all the typical qualities of a victim: they were easy prey for calumny, often wealthy and never armed. The German nation, refusing to believe in its own defeat after 1918, accepted with enthusiasm the doctrine of the "Jewish revolution" which was supposed to have frustrated Germany's victory.

"Acts of barbarism, defying all description, have been committed on Jews by Germans of all classes—well-educated, supposedly enlightened people among them"—so Hugo Marx had summed up what has happened. Of course the ghastly spectacle of the sacking and annihilation of German Jewry filled a number of Germans with disgust; and some even tried to help their Jewish friends. But not the masses. A questionnaire I have sent out to Jewish refugees in this country confirmed in 90 per cent of all cases sampled the active participation, or at least connivance, in pogroms on the part of the German masses. I know of only one verified case of a German Gentile who dared to stand up and defend a persecuted Jew.

I have from a German Jew the story of a Gentile friend of his turned Nazi who came to him after the great pogroms of 1938. "I can't shake hands with you," said he, "mine has just set fire to your synagogue." That episode is typical of the confusion of German emotional life: one does his duty as a barbarian, and at the same time is ashamed of it before his friend. Indeed, for Germany's greater glory such a man would kill his own brother—and then sit down and weep.

The meanest crime of all seems to me the Nazi decree which erased the names of the Jewish soldiers from the marble tablets small German towns erected in memory of local citizens killed in action.

But whatever our contempt for such meanness, it is equaled by our feelings concerning Jews who accepted the status of "honorary Aryan"—von Oppenheim, von Weinberg, Air Marshal Milch, and others. The author Arnold Bronnen may lay claim to a special rank in that category: he brought evidence to court that an Aryan had sired him in adultery with his Gentile mother.

A lot of Jewish leaders in Germany have acted with a heroism worthy of Jewish exploits in all great national crises. The chief rabbi of Berlin, Beck, turned down a passport to leave Germany and so refused to save his own skin, as the Kaiser had done. The head of the

Warsaw ghetto chose suicide rather than carry out an order to deliver several hundred of his coreligionists to the Nazis.

In twelve years not a single Gentile has risen in Germany to express his feelings about the horrors inflicted upon the Jews. There is indeed not the slightest evidence that the age-old anti-Jewish suspicion of the Germans will ever wane. The German-Jewish split is incurable.

Part Two

I have often felt a bitter pang at the thought of the German people, so estimable as individuals, so wretched in the whole. GOETHE

6 THE LAST LESSON

FOR TWENTY YEARS the world, and above all the American world, has been deceived by German propaganda. Here are two principal lies that Americans, with the exception of a few thousand people, have taken for the truth.

1. Wilson's promises, embodied in his Fourteen Points, induced the High Command to surrender in 1918.

2. It was the obstinacy of French demands which, supported by England, weakened the German republic; thus German finances were destroyed by billions of reparation payments, which, in turn, put millions of German workers out of work.

These falsifications were disseminated by truly devilish means. The conquest of American compassion was the first concern—and soon was the first success—of the German peace republic, which had been enforced upon that warrior nation against its will. The United States was the most powerful country among Germany's former enemies, and this was the reason for Germany's concern. There lived as citizens of the United States millions of people of German descent, and some of them paved the road to success. While puritanism had suffered during the war in England, it was still very much alive in America and could be appealed to—this was the secret of Germany's propaganda success.

What did the German republic actually do to achieve these results? In the course of some eight years six hundred German university professors or professors-to-be were sent overseas. Since for the time being Germany was, or seemed to be, disarmed—supposedly for good —she lost no time in showing her other face by thus sending overseas the "peaceful spiritual heirs of Goethe and Beethoven." Instead of the sharp-taloned eagle there now appeared the gentle dove; and America could see for herself the "other" Germany which at last had come to the fore. Six hundred propagandists climbed out of a giant Trojan horse and began to disseminate the myths of Germany's innocence in starting the war, of the "stab in the back," and of French vengefulness.

It was the best of all American characteristics, sympathy for the losing party, which made Americans stumble into that pitfall. When in 1928 I tried to restore historic truth, and through lectures and my book *July '14* essayed to warn of the threat of German vengeance, I encountered stern opposition both in universities and government circles; and a part of the press attacked me as a warmonger. The unpopularity of the League—its failure seemed to warrant such feelings —had its share in turning into a "poor victim" the party which before all was guilty of unleashing the war.

American sympathies for France suffered a setback when that country failed to meet its financial obligations; and the creditor did not understand that France was unable to pay as long as Germany did not pay France. Moreover, the war-guilt "confession" which Clemenceau had made the Germans sign ran contrary to the American concept of fair play. It is curious that the American people upheld Wilson's humanitarian principles so strictly in the case of French postwar policies—after they had deserted his noble ideas as a whole and had left the great man to die in despair. It was an ill fate indeed that the country where the League was invented destroyed it by refraining from joining it. Now their decision was growing doubly fateful, because America, aware of the mistake of 1919, had, or was tricked, into a bad conscience. Moreover, it seems that the American can enjoy his victory only when he can shake hands with the losing party after the fight. In short, all psychological factors played into Germany's hands.

Long-standing admiration for German efficiency favored the sentimental wish of some German-American circles to see the country o their ancestors rise in new glory. Germany's vitality and prospects seemed great, and her inventions, industries, and shipping lines promised good business to boot—provided she could be talked out of her ancient lust for war. Only France became unpopular.

When France withdrew her troops from the Rhineland five years ahead of time, no one seemed to remember that, fifty years earlier, the Germans after their French victory had not withdrawn their army of occupation a minute ahead of full payment of French reparations. But most Americans took French generosity in the case of the Rhineland occupation as a matter of course—as did the Germans themselves. When the news of the early Rhineland evacuation reached Germany, a so-called Liberal said to me with a grin, "You see your Frenchmen? Despicable weaklings—that's what they are!" In that moment I realized what today, seventeen years later, I want to sum up as a warning: If you do a German a favor he at once takes it for granted and asks for twice as much.

German propaganda found a helpmate in the shortsightedness of American bankers, who began to do business with Germany. Today they realize the enormity of their mistake. I asked three leading bankers why they had granted those loans. "Perhaps we *are* to blame for the second war," the first said; "without us the Germans would not have been able to rearm." The second only mentioned the large commissions American bankers were after; and the third said, "We did it because we had too much idle money." According to American figures, Germans borrowed about six billion dollars from Allied sources in the twenties, and paid about four billion in reparations; how much they repaid on loans is a matter of contention. But in any case they were the only party to profit financially from the war. And who lost all that money? Not merely a few big operators, whose loss would have been only what they deserved, but the American public.

The falsification of history was in the main put into practice through those six hundred "scholars" the German republic sent out for that very purpose; from their lectures and publications the myth made its way into American periodicals and books. For twenty-odd years German propaganda succeeded in making *unknown* the following facts to the majority of the American public:

Up to 1930 the fact that Hindenburg and Ludendorff had manipulated the German surrender themselves was practically unknown to the general public. As early as the 29th of September 1918 (four weeks before the sailors-and-workers revolt) the two generals had virtually given up by recommending an armistice "within twenty-four hours." It was unknown, too, that these two generals were the ones to ask for a democratic government, and overnight enforced a parliamentary system—"to get Wilson's Fourteen Points," as they cynically put it according to the files.

Most Americans did not realize that Germany had not surrendered because she really put her trust in Wilson, but solely because she was licked; nor that Prussian Junkers and generals were not in the habit of defending the fatherland.

In the twenties German propaganda sought to hide the fact that France, half destroyed, lay on the ground while Germany brilliantly recovered at top speed, fed by those very foreign loans which France did not get. They enjoyed the fact that practically all German plants were at work from 1924 to 1928, new ships were launched, and chemical and optical industries experienced a boom.

But when the world depression set in in 1929, with five millions of unemployed in Germany against much more in this country, German propaganda, shifting between wrath and tears, had an easy job in convincing American public opinion that what happened to them was but a consequence of Anglo-French ill will. Another few years, and Hitler's rise was accounted for through the two statements that a desperate country, harassed by avid victors, was throwing itself into the arms of the first adventurer to come its way, and that Germans felt they were called upon to save "European culture from the Communist barbarians." German propaganda told the Americans that Germany was a new St. George setting out to kill the dragon, Russia. Hitler's success was based upon that faith; even today it is often used in favor of the German enemy and as a warning against the Russian ally.

The traveler approaching New York Harbor first sees the Statue of Liberty; entering the center of Berlin he beholds the victory chariot on the Brandenburger Tor, and close by the Victory Column. Germany is the only country which lacks both a hero of liberty and a monument to liberty. Some Germans gave their lives in the struggle against Napoleon; their names are generally unknown, except perhaps that of the Tyrolese peasant Andreas Hofer, who grew to be a popular figure. But men who might have risen against their tyrannical princes, the kind who live both in the history and the hearts of all other countries including Russia, exist neither in German history nor in German legend. To ascertain the names of the men who died in the short-lived Berlin revolution of 1848 the traveler has to find the memorial tablet to them in a cemetery.

The first German revolution was betrayed by Luther in 1525; the second was quelled by the kings in 1848 after a few weeks; the third, in 1918, was no revolution. The shift of power from the Junkers to the citizenry came off with practically no loss of life on either side. For three hundred solid years many thousands of army officers had enjoyed all sorts of privileges under the royal pennant; but when their royalism was put to test in 1918 not more than two officers gave their lives for that flag: Lieutenants Zenker and Weniger, commoners both. The third martyr was an aged general who, stricken by grief, committed suicide in front of the Bismarck monument at Goslar. Once in those days I happened to watch some army officers in a Berlin trolley car as enlisted men cut off their insignia; there was no violence —simply because these officers did not offer the slightest resistance.

The German revolution produced a phenomenon unique in world history: officers and Junkers, the hereditary paladins of the Hohenzollern king, broke faith the moment he left—while the only ones who kept faith after the king's flight were the plain citizens, the people. With the ancient awe in their hearts they appeared before their ruling princes—if indeed these gentlemen had not run away before—and full of embarrassment implored them to leave. When the terror-stricken crown princess did not dare leave her Potsdam castle, dreading to share the tsarina's fate, a group of soldiers entered her room, and one of them said in a military tone, "Her Imperial Highness is under our protection. We are waiting for her orders."

Not the slightest harm was done to any of the twenty-two German kings and princelings, their sons, nephews, or cousins. Not a single soldier or worker threatened their lives, or touched their dignity. Four weeks after the revolution I traveled the small capitals of their principalities: everywhere people hastened to assure me that their grand duke had been the last to give in when at last he had to abdicate. Only one, the Duke of Waldeck, saved the show by declaring that, besides being the ruler of Waldeck, he also was "Sovereign of Pyrmont." Whereupon his subjects called him The Stubborn, until he, too, had finally to make his exit.

That revolution against everybody's will has indeed no counterpart in world history. If ruling princes and Junkers had really possessed those virtues they accredited to themselves, five hundred stouthearted army officers could have saved royalty in 1918. But the point was that in their core not a thousand Germans were genuine anti-monarchists; the Socialists themselves did not lift a finger to overthrow the monarchy. The princes ran away from the people whose obedience they underrated, while the people, underrating the princes' cowardice, were deadly afraid of them. This, then, was the German revolution.

Only the sailors of a number of warships showed determination. On November 5 they refused to sacrifice their lives for a lost cause. And these were their demands: release of their jailed comrades; equal food rations with officers; no saluting when off duty; and a change in the awkward German military form of addressing a superior. Hard as it is to believe, these were the only demands of eighty thousand sailors who had three thousand officers in their power.

The discipline of workers' councils was such that Hindenburg himself felt prompted to support that revolutionary institution—whereupon some of them presently admitted officers to membership. In Königsberg a group of these "admitted" officers sent the workers forty-four geese as a token of their appreciation. Nothing shows better the prevalence in Germany of order before freedom even under the most chaotic conditions than an incident in Hamburg; there the Socialists found the trade-union building occupied by a group of workers more radical than they themselves; but instead of dislodging them by force, they persuaded a judge of the old regime to sign an order of eviction—which, after due presentation to the radical group, brought about its exodus. The siege of the Berlin *Marstall* by Ebert's troops was interrupted when the latter made a truce with the entrenched sailors; it was Christmas; after the holidays fighting would be resumed.

Here is another significant episode. When news of the German revolution reached the lunch table in the German embassy at Petrograd, one of the lackeys could not help overhearing the message. He was very embarrassed indeed, for he felt that now he alone represented the German people. According to an eyewitness, who told it to me, the servant made up his mind neither to play the revolutionist nor to pretend to have heard nothing; steering a typical German middle course, he took off his white gloves and went on serving at table without them.

Quite similarly the German nation went on serving its masters, though without the white gloves of imperial days. While the pillars of public order were changed, everything went on with the old punctuality. Rumors had it that drunken sailors wallowed on the beds of the Kaiser and his spouse; when I looked over the place on December 28, 1918, the sailor in charge of the famous *Weisser Saal* showed me a number of broken panes, and apologized for their not having been repaired yet. Then he proceeded to point out to me three orderly piles of litter below the windows: one of masonry and bricks, another one formed by metalwork from the building, and a third pile of broken glass.[1]

Like that litter the citizenry of Germany formed three orderly though battle-scarred factions: the old power, the new forces, and the radicals. The question in that revolution was not which party had more courage, but which had less fear than the two others. Since their barricades were not built of cobblestones but by the different patterns of Weltanschauung, the dash and daring which decide the fate of revolutions were missing.

Only where the radicals were shot at was there much action. The uneven fight of two factions against one decided at once the downfall of the Weimar republic. The men who died for liberty in January 1919 were not victims of the defeated royalists, but victims of their own brethren. The fight between Socialists and the so-called Spartacists (Communists) destroyed hundreds of lives—and with them also the lives of the two genuine heroes of the German revolution, Liebknecht and Rosa Luxemburg. They were killed with the connivance of their comrades.

In fact, German Socialists had wanted neither a revolution nor a republic. They had always been petty bourgeois. In fifty years they had only two important leaders. Forming numerically the greatest chapter of the Socialist International, they had yet remained without any original ideas. Nowhere were German Rightists so wrong as in honoring the German Socialists by calling them "November criminals."

When on October 5, 1918, the dispossessed Junker class forced democracy upon Socialists and Liberals, the Socialist leadership was stupid or, as they termed it, patriotic enough to accept the legacy instead of turning it down. Thus they shouldered the responsibility for the armistice that concluded a war which, though they had partic-

[1] I happened to be the only civilian to see those three truly symbolic piles, and described the sight in print the following day. The boycott of the republic I described as early as March 1919 in the book *An die Laterne.*

ipated in it, they themselves had certainly neither unleashed nor led.

Even in the very last days before the Kaiser's flight Socialist leaders kept on declaring they wanted no violence of any sort. On November 9, when the Communists rose and the Independent Socialist Liebknecht, standing on one of the balconies of the royal castle, proclaimed the republic, the Socialists felt themselves the dupes of their rivals. A few minutes later Scheidemann, one of them, wanted to duplicate the show by proclaiming the republic in his turn from another balcony. Ebert ran after him, and in the presence of about a hundred members of the old Reichstag shouted, "You have no right to do anything of this kind! It's up to the National Assembly to decide the future form of government!" Ebert that very morning had in vain urged Prince Max von Baden to remain in office as chancellor; Germans could not even conceive of a free country without some princely protection, just as they did in Frankfurt in 1848.

The course of events had compelled Ebert to assume office over night. The following day he made a deal with Field Marshal von Hindenburg—first by telephone, and then in writing. Whereas freedom-loving nations have so often imprisoned or executed rulers who led them into disaster, the new leaders of Germany made a pact with them, and thus crippled the body of the infant republic at the very moment of its birth.

These first steps were decisive. So long as a defeated adversary is still afraid of violence, he has at least some respect for the new power. But when he remains unharmed in a comfortable hideout, awaiting dangers which do not materialize, he is bound to step forth again soon, touch his old pal on the shoulder, and say, "Where there's nothing to be afraid of, there's everything to gain."

The ultimate cause of the failure of the German revolution lies in German awe of the uniform. Only he who has a sword has power. All of these Socialist schoolteachers, workers' sons, and proletarians had carried rifles during the war, but, seldom getting commissions, they had never had a sword. Now they felt flattered when generals with broad red stripes on their trousers and glittering decorations on their chests stooped down to them in loyalty and almost-friendship. These one-time enlisted men were now in a position to address the exalted gentlemen as excellencies, and if their legs and arms did not stand at attention, their hearts surely did. Some of them did not mind being addressed as excellencies themselves in their new ministerial offices. In short, they adopted the very attitude of those who for a few centuries plus four years had despised them. They were not after money; with one single exception the Socialist officials of the Weimar republic cannot be accused of graft. Again you see what the German yearns for is power, social acknowledgment, titles; not money.

What the Socialists really wanted was to be taken seriously. When those worldly counts and barons, who up to the last minute had commandeered both army and State, swallowed their pride for a few short months and mixed with the "sons of the people," the latter, far from looking through the makeshift, began to extol the old generals. Details of that kind of co-operation later reached the public through the farcical scenes of a political trial; some of it I have included in my Hindenburg book.

The old excellencies, real princes among them, invited the proletarian-born Minister of Defense to dinner at their club, and dined and wined with him so long and so intensively that in the end they managed to grill the good man himself on the point of their swords, and devour him to the last morsel. When one of the notorious *Freikorps* one day paraded before Ebert, his Minister of Defense said to him (according to an eyewitness' memoirs): "Don't worry, Fritz, everything will be in order again!"

Of all appropriations asked for in the Reichstag only the army appropriation escaped interference by the opposition during fourteen years. Behind the Minister of Defense and the appropriation there stood the Reichswehr generals—the old generals of the late imperial army. When fourteen million Germans voted in a plebiscite for expropriation of the runaway Kaiser, the Socialists—who really should have led the motion—killed it by not casting their votes; apparently they were embarrassed at the idea that so distinguished a cavalier as their one-time political adversary—who, incidentally, had long before transferred abroad a good half of his fortune—should be exposed to "starvation."

All Germans knew of, and sanctioned, secret rearmament. Six or eight years before Hitler, classrooms all over the country displayed maps which contrasted the German 1918 frontiers to what they would be again. Both the French General Nollet and the English Brigadier General Morgan, chief of the Disarmament Commission, later presented in print the utter hopelessness of their mission in the face of such general popular connivance at rearmament.

The new German generals, who were the old German generals, had an easy game to play. For two hundred years the Germans had been accustomed to soldiering in war and peace; they were only too happy to get new soldiers from Santa Claus. At the height of the separatist crisis of 1923 in Bavaria, Ebert asked General von Seeckt at a cabinet meeting, "Are you sure the troops will be behind the government?" "In any case they'll be behind me," von Seeckt retorted, fixing his monocle in his eye. He was neither imprisoned nor demoted. A gifted soldier, he was generally admired. It was, incidentally, von Seeckt who coined the expression, *Der Tag,* meaning the day of revenge.

Lust for revenge was a general feeling in Germany. Instead of hating those whose arrogance and incompetence had led them into disaster, people concentrated their hatred on the victors. That reaction, to be sure, would have been understandable had they been at the mercy of victors who enslaved them as they themselves had enslaved Rumania and Russia in the peace treaties of 1917 and 1918. But the victorious powers were under the influence of Wilsonian humanism, and had offered peace on fairer terms than were offered by most previous treaties in modern times. Except for those territories which Germany had taken by force in former wars, all territorial changes were subject to plebiscites. In acknowledgment of that fairness the

Germans falsified the results of plebiscites. My mother, who was born in Upper Silesia but had not returned there for fifty years, was asked to travel there (ticket paid) and vote in the plebiscite—and this she did.

Added to this may be the farce of the reparation payments. The German Government drew up an account of "payments already made," including such items as the scuttled navy and unpaid labor of German prisoners of war—in toto a bill for sixty-seven billion dollars. Allied calculations arrived at a sum of twenty billions. Even if one accepts the German figures for reparations paid, and does not discount foreign loans received, these alleged billion dollars paid do not represent more than 1.7 per cent of the Reich's national income in the period payments. In fact, the Germans who day and night protested against the financial provisions of the "slave treaty" and declared they had neither cash nor raw materials, only a few years later, without any foreign loan, raised sixty billion marks for Hitler's rearmament.

In the main the German Government escaped reparation payments through manipulated inflation (or, rather, fraudulent bankruptcy) by which it got rid of all internal debts; and through the "failure" to prevent enormous private funds from being illegally transferred abroad.

After the signing of the slave treaty industrial shares began to go up, and kept on going up throughout the period of reparation payments.

Some years after 1918 a Prussian prince was auctioning off his possessions—which included a flute that had belonged to Frederick the Great. A group of Potsdam army officers decided to save the Hohenzollern relic from that humiliation. They informed the prince of their intention, threatening to "protect as one man the flute of the great king." Whereupon the prince answered coolly, "If on November 9, 1918, you gentlemen had protected your king with equal determination, there would be no need today to auction the flute." Like the Reich itself, the famous flute passed into bourgeois hands.

But these bourgeois and proletarians had neither experience nor talent. The only one who showed both, Walther Rathenau, was assassinated after five months in office. What these new rulers lacked was a Siberia which would have nurtured and matured their revolutionary attitude, the Tsarist jails which would have trained them in underground work. The only solid backing they had was in trade unions built along military lines; German union men loved to sing the old songs which glorified the beautiful army years of their youth. Political talent was sadly stunted by dictatorship of fifty years' standing, whether bearing the name of Bismarck, the Kaiser, or Ludendorff. Thus these new "leaders of the people" were neither good speakers nor bargainers, and soon called in their better experienced adversaries whose families had for two hundred years been trained in governmental technique. And the new men did not notice how soon they were taken in. Every Junker family tried to get at least one of its members into the administration or higher civil service; not in vain did they expect each of these men to look after the interests of a hundred other Junkers. In 1913 the proportion of noblemen in the Prussian officers' corps was 22 per cent against 21.3 in the republican year of 1921. The missing 0.7 per cent apparently represented the victorious revolution.

The new leaders had not learned how to use their power; and were afraid to use it. They resembled a troupe of actors who overnight have to take on the leading parts in a show whose original cast has been marooned en route. Immediately after the collapse, the old German passion for legitimate order took on definitely nationalistic accents. Every one tried to appear as patriotic as possible. Had not labor for fifty years been smirched as "the class without a fatherland"? Now was the moment to gain legitimacy! Now the old Reich against which they had fought for so long appeared to them in its full glory. "Reich," not republic, became the current term for Germany. As people abroad translated "Reich" as "empire," they came to feel how little had changed in Germany. It was not long before the new colors of the republic were so bitterly hated in Germany that the display of flags on the streets had to be forbidden by decree to protect the colors of the republic from ridicule. It occurred to no one in the government that the dignity of national colors might be protected in displaying them.

Yet there was a certain tendency to keep face. Following a time-honored pattern, the government assigned a parliamentary commission to investigate the causes for Germany's defeat. When that committee had the audacity to summon Hindenburg and Ludendorff, the field marshal's trip to Berlin was made a national holiday by university students. For the first time in German history a high-ranking, decorated nobleman faced a people's tribunal—although this court really only wanted to question, not to try him. Six questions were put to Hindenburg; he had got them in writing beforehand. One of them concerned the unrestricted U-boat war he had pressed in spite of American warnings, another the notorious hurry of the High Command in asking for the armistice.

But Hindenburg was not prepared to answer questions. He had come to accuse. With his roaring bass voice he began to read from his papers a presentation of the innocence of the Kaiser's government in declaring war. Then he turned to a glorification of the four years of victory. When the chairman tried to interrupt him, the field marshal scarcely paused in the reading of his paper. Three times the gavel broke in—three times the people's impatient voice reached his ear. And three times the defendant calmly proceeded—until he finally came to talk of "those criminal machinations which attacked the victorious army in the rear. From the rear," he concluded, "the army was assassinated."

The Liberal chairman was enormously relieved when it was all over and he was no longer forced to raise the gavel. No one in the Reichstag dared refute Hindenburg's calumnies. On his trip home thousands cheered the field marshal. Six years later he was elected to the presidency of the republic.

That election was a revealing symptom. For the first time in a thousand years the Germans were called upon to choose their own chief of state, and among all the courageous and vigorous men who were available none suited them as a leader. They chose an old general who affirmed that the old glory of Germany should be restored; means: revenge.

Soon his presidency was to become a tragic farce, for he said about the League, "A people with as much as a drop of manly blood in its veins will never submit its national honor to arbitration by foreigners." As it was, no one could blame an old soldier for clinging to the traditions of his past rather than relying on the uncertain values of the future. The nation which elected him is to blame—the same nation which hated the idea of a league.

Yet Hindenburg's election was a less decisive factor than it may seem. Neither the Catholic candidate nor, for that matter, anyone else, if elected, could have made anything of a policy of anti-rearmament. For rearmament and revenge were what the whole German nation wanted.

After 1918 there is abundant proof of that tendency in public opinion, particularly in Germany's intellectual life. What German propaganda had to build up artificially in America was taken as a matter of course at hime. In a specific sense advocates of the "Versailles guilt" theory are right. The Versailles Treaty *is* to be blamed: its fatal drawback was not to be the "Potsdam Treaty." To halt the Allied armies against General Pershing's advice, and not to march on and dictate the treaty on German soil—this was a fatal weakness. France would never have believed she had been defeated had the victors of 1814, 1871, and 1940 not paraded through the streets of Paris. But in 1918 no foreign uniform demonstrated to the Germans their defeat. A victor who signs the peace treaty in his own capital city without occupying the enemy's is more than likely to arouse that enemy's contempt—and most certainly so if it is the Germans who are defeated.

The German people had seen enemy troops in only two small border sections of their country and only in the first weeks of the war; they had not been bombed; later none of the ruling princes or generals had been made to answer the people's questions when all was lost. No wonder they refused to believe in their defeat. *The Unvanquished Army* or *The German Navy Was Never Beaten*—these were the titles of books sold by hundreds of thousands. Instead, anyone who dared to say or write the truth was ostracized. In those days F. W. Foerster, one of the noblest living Germans, now in New York, editor of a pacifist magazine, received many letters from his subscribers asking him to mail his material in sealed envelopes—lest neighbors should see it.

All this was not in 1933—it happened in 1921, the third year of the republic. Whoever ventured to expose the secret rearmament that was going on was accused of treason and often convicted—as later happened to Ossietzky, who was to receive the Nobel peace prize. As an exile the former Chancellor Wirth explicitly protested against Hitler's boasts of having been the one to rearm Germany—he began it himself in 1922, but had been forced to keep his mouth shut.

In fact, the whole nation was in on the secret. Every German medical or bar association contributed regularly to mysterious "funds" whose treasurers did not even render account of their budget.

No, the Germans had learned nothing from their defeat. They could not, because they denied its existence—denied it in the face of two million dead and five million cripples. And yet their foremost, if not their only, thought was revenge.

These phenomena reveal a basic difference from the Italian attitude. Germans have always rejected freedom and craved victory—while Italians strive for liberty and sometimes boycott victory. This is why Mussolini was tolerated later on and Hitler deified. For forty-four years the Italians fought for their liberation; fighting, they gained national unity. During centuries which never witnessed a German upheaval Italians rose time and again in every part of their country. Americans of the occupation army will understand Romans much better than Berliners; for with the former they share their love of freedom.

Mussolini[2] once said to me with a sigh, "Yes, if it were Germans I had to rule!" He realized the deep sense of independence in his own countrymen, and envied a future German dictator who would find a ready-made docile and flexible "material." After as long as twenty years he could not help tolerating in his senate so important a democrat as Benedetto Croce. Neither the best leaders of the Italian intelligentsia nor Roman Society ever yielded to the Duce. Actually, it was in good taste to make anti-Fascist remarks.

In Germany ten years *before* Hitler the opposite was taking place. The few Germans who wanted their country to remain disarmed and to concentrate on its industrial and intellectual potentialities were persecuted. Let me offer some little episodes from my own experiences.

I published an article in a Swiss newspaper urging the German generals accused of war crimes to go to Paris and face trial; whereupon the *Völkischer Beobachter,* which had just come into existence, threatened me with death unless I left the country at once. That happened in the second year of the republic: 1920!

In 1926 the principal of a high school recommended my book on the Kaiser to his students; he was promptly dismissed by the republican government.

Another symptom of the true spirit of the Weimar republic was the collapse of German pacifism at the very time when that movement gained momentum abroad.

As in all countries, the Socialists were also pacifists in imperial Germany. But once in the republican government themselves, they

[2]My book *Talks with Mussolini,* published in 1932, before he began his wars, contains no comment on Fascist Italy which would go as far as Churchill's enthusiasm up to 1938. Contrary to rumor, I never wrote a Mussolini biography. What I did was to converse *in antithetical fashion* with a Fascist—as his democratic antipode. Some of his statements were so far from the Fascist philosophy that the Italian anti-Fascists quoted him, but his friends came to him, the Pope sent to him to tell him the danger of this book. So he suppressed the book *six days after its publication;* only after drastic changes he made later, was the book authorized again, against my protest. I never saw him again. I have nothing to recant of what I wrote in 1932 and nothing of what I wrote for thirty years.

changed their policies. For forty years they had frustrated the Kaiser's naval ambitions because of the imperialistic dangers implied; but the Socialist Chancellor Mueller countersigned the appropriation for the first new pocket cruiser. At a time when English Socialists still did not perceive the German peril and continued to vote for disarmament, their German Socialist brethren not only accepted rearmament but in 1931 went so far as to forbid their party members to join the "German Peace Society."

Since their establishment by Lassalle, German labor associations (*Arbeitervereine*) had carried on the fight against colonies, armament, and provocative foreign politics. If it was in vain, it was still a demonstration; neither personal sacrifices nor penalties had weakened their determination on that score. But in 1914 they went off to war with enthusiasm, and most of their parliamentarians voted for all the war appropriations. In both cases they referred to a stupid remark of their leader Bebel, who had said, "If it is against the Tsar, I'll shoulder a rifle myself and march off!"

In World War I one of the labor leaders wrote, "Air bombardment is an excellent device to terrorize civilians behind the front. And terror is humane, for it shortens the war." And the prominent Liberal Catholic leader maintained that it would be "more humane to destroy the whole of London than to sacrifice the life of a single German combatant."

The handful of genuine, active German pacifists, younger men most of them, who formed a "peace cartel" were everywhere shunned as pariahs. One of the best books of these years, *Germany's Tragedy,* had at first to be published anonymously. *Der Untertan,* by Heinrich Mann, the best of all literary treatments of the modern German character, written in 1913, was not published until 1919.

And what did the old Reichstag do in the most crucial months, that is, from the collapse to the first meeting of the National Assembly? It had gone on vacation, and was heard of only once: on December 1 1918, its speaker protested to the new government against the cancella tion of the passes on government-owned railroads enjoyed by members of the Reichstag.

All classes and political parties were unanimous in their unconcern about possible German war guilt and their concern about the guilt of the Allies. No one wanted to acknowledge that the system as such had been wrong. Rightists and Leftists joined hands in maintaining that they had been cheated by America, and that they were and remained the real victors in the war. Nothing was changed in the administrative apparatus. *Geheimräte* (permanent secret councilors) were, or seemed to be, irremovable; they kept the reins in their hands, and graciously permitted the new parliamentary ministers to deliver speeches. They knew well that a barrel if not well scraped will always smell of the old vintage, whatever new wine it may contain. And this was precisely what they wanted. First of all they did their best to spare the old nobility any hardship. Most of the flunkies of the twenty-two courts got their pensions. The old "landed property districts" (*Gutsbezirke*), basis of local Junker influence, remained unchanged as administrative bodies. No one was astonished when the owners of estates that had been ceded to Poland in the peace treaty hastened to acquire Polish citizenship; on the contrary, it was, so people said, all for the good of German national rights abroad. In order to compromise the new German colors, the navy retained the old imperial flag besides.

All this was done with the consent of the new Liberal leaders. But it was neither money nor personal interest which bribed them. The old classes, their cavalier's deportment, their dinner jackets, soon corrupted the new men. These upstart artisans, printers, sergeants, and party secretaries had spent a lifetime waiting in the antechambers of their high-born compatriots; now they, too, at last wanted to be able to show the easy smile, the light tone, and the good manners of those gentlemen—and did not realize that any smart waiter could learn it all in no time. Because European protocol forced kings to appear in public on horseback, the first president of the republic elected by the Assembly, a former harness maker, and a man of fifty years, learned how to ride. Some others engaged in sports; and some tried the bon ton at garden parties of the new banking magnates. Instead of sitting behind the wheel of the tractor to plow the field of the new epoch, they picked the late flowers of the nineteenth century.

The real public life of the republic was dulled by a complete lack of imagination. And certainly the spirit of a newly organized country cannot thrive without new symbols. But we who kept on suggesting new emblems or new songs got nothing but ridicule. For it was exactly the old ones the Germans wanted.

One of the most popular motifs in the general concert of hate was Germany's "partition." How often do Americans mention to me the Polish Corridor as one of the reasons for Hitler's rise to power! In fact that ill-famed "Corridor" which separated East Prussia from the rest of the country was of no greater harm to Germany than British Columbia is to this country in separating the states from the Territory of Alaska. Actually, it was only a number of Junker families with possessions in the Corridor who suffered—financially. Born near the Polish border, I came soon to learn how little known these eastern regions were in the rest of the Reich; I was asked by Rhineland people, long before World War I, whether my family's native town Gleiwitz did not belong to Polish Russia.

The Rhineland is the only real popular area among the German provinces. The Rhine is the background of the old legends; it is the habitat of German wine, the birthplace of German *Lieder,* and the eternal battlefield of Germans and Frenchmen. Neither Alsace nor Posen nor Schleswig (to mention a few of the contested provinces with mixed populations) mean much to German feeling in general; Thuringia, Frankfurt, Franconia, Bavaria, Baden—these age-old, beautiful German holdings are really popular.

I was a witness to some ironical private remarks of high-ranking German foreign office men when in September 1926 Stresemann had at last succeeded in convincing first himself and then his colleagues of the advisability of Germany's joining the League. But that attitude was far from being limited to Junker circles and the budding Nazi party; deep in the whole nation there lived a distrust of any kind of international co-operation. Certainly it is even stronger today. Field Marshal von Moltke voiced only what every German thought when he said, "Perpetual peace is a dream, and not even a beautiful one." How can one love peace and fight at the same time—and fight not as in a contest but as in war? A pacified Europe seems unmanly to the German. For a hundred years he has regarded each war as a link in a chain of wars, and each "peace" only as a limited truce, even after victory. Perpetual peace, so he has felt, was all right for philosophers who quite obviously didn't know anything about life anyway.

As their class had done for the past seventy years, German university teachers vied with one another in their anti-Europeanism. Unlike their English and French colleagues, many of whom had still supported the value of German scholarship in the midst of World War I, German scholars had already at that time rejected the idea of international values. No other than the aged Ernst Haeckel, then the best known of German savants, had written, "A single highly civilized German soldier such as unfortunately perishes now by the thousands represents a hundredfold greater spiritual and moral value than hundreds of the uneducated children of nature who face his kind in England, France, Russia, or Italy." To such depth the foremost biologist of his time has stooped. He had been an upright man all his life, as little afraid of the Church as Luther; but, like Luther, he was afraid of the State.

It did not need defeat to turn German professors into nationalists; but defeat made real jingoes of them. Aside from a dozen or so excellent men who dared to teach historic truth the five thousand-odd professors seemed to be united in a secret agreement to teach youth the myth of the unvanquished army, and arouse them against the republic. A college teacher who joined a peace meeting risked his position; if he contributed to one of the few independent periodicals he was dismissed.

When I investigated the documents on the outbreak of the first war, and in my book *July '14* tried to distribute the war guilt among Vienna, Berlin, and St. Petersburg, Liberal historians all over the country accused me of high treason, and the most prominent Liberal paper, the Frankfurter *Zeitung,* attacked the book on its publication.

The worst feature of the republic's policy of camouflage was its scheme to commission certain hand-picked scholars to prove the historical righteousness of what they wanted to have proved. Thus Herr Haushofer, a university professor who was in fact an army general, invented "geopolitics," and presently made that science the basis for general staff studies.

From university chairs the patriotic defense of the lie invaded the highest courts. It was the Americans and the Japanese who first prevented the extradition of fifteen hundred war criminals who, according to the peace treaty, were to be arraigned for thirty-two different crimes. American jurists declared the "laws of humanity" to be "too vague" as a legal basis for their prosecution; and as to the Kaiser they quoted an opinion of Chief Justice Marshall dating from 1812 that no sovereign could possibly be arraigned. The Dutch Government, which had given refuge to the Kaiser, got a hint from London, and presently rejected the official demand for extradition.

Encouraged by that first success, the Germans began to clamor for the right to try their war criminals before German courts; and the very signers of the treaty which stipulated extradition were not ashamed of joining that chorus of indignation. The Allies gave in, dropped six hundred names from the original list, and delivered the files of the remaining nine hundred to the Reich Supreme Court in Leipzig—a body which once enjoyed as much esteem in the world as the United States Supreme Court. In eight hundred and eighty-two cases the Reich Court without arraignment or trial declared the accused not guilty. They arraigned fourteen. There were actual trials for only four officers who had torpedoed hospital ships, fired at lifeboats, et cetera. An army general who in the first weeks of the war had ordered all prisoners killed was acquitted on the ground that his order was "apparently based on a misunderstanding." Of the four officers who were finally convicted, two served six months' terms; the other two "escaped" from prison. The whole nation, including the press of all political shades, was elated. Not a single German jurist, pastor, or university professor protested, and I had to defend the republic abroad.

With Junkers and university teachers, who are first of all to be blamed for the downfall of the republic, a third class joined forces: the leading industrialists. It was those Kirdorffs, Krupps, Duisbergs, Bosches, Thyssens, Stinneses, and Voegelers who—at the people's expense—made their profit from Germany's defeat. Long before Hitler this pressure group fostered rearmament, which provided their plants with profitable contracts. They also financed the notorious Freikorps, which was to form the nucleus of the new army. They supported the Black Reichswehr, and made possible those sinister organizations which murdered so many, two cabinet ministers among them. In their laboratories new brands of poison gas were invented long before Hitler, and sold to Japan. The I.G.F. offered and later delivered its chemical secrets to Mussolini, and thus forced Italian chemical concerns into partnership. As early as 1931 Herr Duisberg could openly declare that "only an economic bloc from Odessa to Bordeaux can secure Europe's world position." The I.G.F.'s lawyer in France was Laval.

Of all modern dictators Hitler is the only one who has gained power by legal means. Napoleon I, Napoleon III, Lenin, and Mussolini have all used armed formations to conquer the capital, dispossess the government, and dissolve what popular representation there was. After their downfall their nations had still a certain right to claim they had been "raped." Hitler knew the passionate love of order and obedience which reigns in the heart of every German; he furthermore knew that Germany had never experienced a successful revolution. Thus he patiently waited two years until he could be sure of election results in his favor. He was not to be disillusioned. When the Germans in March and November 1932, in their two last free elections, had their choice among eight principal parties, twelve million votes went to the Nazis against seven million that were cast for the Socialists. Hitler had openly displayed his political program, and these twelve million knew what he wanted; by voting for him they gave their consent, and clearly expressed their wish to see him in power. A similar landslide had no parallel in German parliamentary history. But even the 44 per cent of all seats the Nazis had gained in the preceding election—thus remaining a minority still—were more than any other single party had ever bagged before.

Of William II the Germans could say they had received him as the heir to the throne; they also could point out in their own favor that the Kaiser had been in a position to declare war without their consent. But the "Führer" they chose freely; their preference for Nazi ideas is thus clear. Indeed, no president in American history rode to Capitol Hill with more legal right than Hitler on his way to the Wilhelmstrasse on January 30, 1933. By legal means he had become chancellor, appointed by Hindenburg on the ground of the numerical strength of his party in parliament. Later, when he was in power, he abused it, destroying every law and constitution, as nobody before him had done.

But Hitler was more than the legal chief of the Germans: he was also their moral head. They never had a more suitable leader. Like a savior he came to those Germans who were so utterly bored and so deadly tired of compulsory self-determination. First of all, he gave to that warrior nation authority, that feature of public life they had so much missed in republican days. At last there was an end to that colorless, paradeless regime in mufti! At last that time without obedience was over! Hitler's real success began with military caps, insignia by the million—and of course without horses; riding boots for his followers, the high boot, as a German symbol of manliness, knighthood, and shining armor, was the first sign of dawning world conquest.

Hitler appeared to most Germans as a combination of Frederick the Great and Lohengrin, with a steel helmet instead of the swan helmet. Even before assuming supreme power, Hitler built up a new German pyramid, patterned after the old. He gave the Germans a hundred new titles and ranks—which they might rattle off when talking to each other, and abbreviate on their visiting cards—bolstering the self-assurance of the little man in Germany who received his own value only through the rank others conceded him. Once more that little man had both obedience and military music, discipline and general enthusiasm.

Leaving aside the swindle of the "abrogated slave treaty" of Versailles, Hitler's success was decided by an age-old trick of all rulers who prepare for war: work and bread for all. Unfortunately, full employment seems to be possible nowadays only through armament. Many American admirers of the Hitlerian "miracle" of full employment have meanwhile witnessed a similar miracle in their own country—dissimilar as those two miracles' motives have been: self-defense here, plain aggression there.

Now the two classes which long before Hitler had begun to prepare for war, Junkers and armament manufacturers, shed the mask and joined the party—even though they saw in their new Führer a combination of crackpot and popular entertainer who was drawing people into the show by his jokes. One is tempted to depict the scene of big business and aristocracy hatching their plot over a glass of bordeaux, and deciding to vest that little fool of a "drummer," as they called him, with power to incite the people to war. However, a certain personal magnetism may also have helped the "man of the people" to attract those so-called *Herrenmenschen*. His master stroke in dealing with their class was to trick the old Prussian generals into taking an oath to his proletarian name but a few hours after Hindenburg's death.

Some people in America wondered how an Austrian could start this war. The truth of the matter is that Hitler was born into a German minority of Bohemia which was always bitterly anti-Austrian; their admiration for Prussian sharpness was matched by their contempt for Austrian "blockheads and weaklings." Berlin, not Vienna, was their star. Precisely the fact that neither Hitler himself nor his chieftains are Prussian by descent—and yet were able to prepare for a world war in Berlin—shows where European wars are actually manipulated. Hitler had to make a pilgrimage to Berlin and win over the German General Staff to get his war. A German war was never hatched anywhere else during the last three hundred years.

University professors he won over even more easily. If generals had always been for war, though under a well-born leader, the professors were for a war under whatever leader might appear; in a way leadership of a commoner flattered them, no matter how much this particular commoner despised all learning. It took Mussolini eight years to make the last university professor take the Fascist oath; Hitler achieved the same end in less than eight weeks. When the first news of the atrocities of his regime reached the outside world, twelve hundred German scientists joined in a manifesto, praising the third Reich as a bulwark of "liberty, honor, justice, and peace." In 1914 not more than ninety-seven leading intellectuals had signed a similar pronunciamento—the number now had increased twelve times.

Not a single voice was raised when Heidelberg University displayed in one classroom a sign, "In writing in German a Jew lies," and in the room next door an outstanding Jewish scholar was lecturing (as some still were in the first months of the regime). No German professor spoke up and risked his job; not one of them so much as left when Jewish faculty colleagues or assistants were flogged behind barbed wire.

I sat at my radio in Switzerland in May 1933 when they burned the books in Berlin, including my own. I heard Goebbels' voice: "Burned because of belittlement of great German thinkers!" Exactly a year before a popular edition of my Goethe biography had a record sale.

Let me insert two revealing statements of German refugees I met in Switzerland at that time. A Socialist politician and former bank messenger, summing up his atrocity tale, said with a sigh, "If we had only known in November 1918 that decapitation was allowed!" The other statement came from a man from Stuttgart who one day, entering his bank, saw the clerks dressed up in breeches and riding boots. "My Führer is in Nuremberg today!" one of them said when asked for the reasons for his attire.

Just as in 1918 no German party had risen to gain liberty, so no party was present fourteen years later to defend it. In both cases the destructive forces in the country had stronger bodies and souls than the constructive powers. In October 1918 Liberals and Leftists had done little themselves to rise to power; actually they had been kicked upstairs. In July 1932 they turned back again to the Junkers the power thus gained even before Hitler's chancellorship, in the interregnum of the so-called *Herrenklub*. And in fact the responsibility of the Socialists for the downfall of the republic dates back to the last two years of the Weimar regime. Under Bruening the Socialist bloc voted for government appropriations together with the Nazis, thereby deciding parliamentary results. And in 1933 the German trade unions "co-ordinated."

For the King of Prussia three army officers gave their lives; no worker gave his life for the German republic. A number of Socialist cabinet ministers and high officials left their desks "under protest" when an army *putsch* kicked them out. One of them, then president of the police force, demonstrated his mental quality later by writing in his memoirs, "So I was sitting at my desk, waiting for further developments."

The workers in Berlin and elsewhere in the country were willing to fight, but they were deserted by their leaders—and that desertion compares well with the flight of the Kaiser in 1918. Today as exiles these leaders voice claims to their former positions. They would rather be put to trial if and when they return to Germany. Their own failure to put the Junkers on trial in 1918 laid the foundations for everything that followed. In the twelve years of the Hitler regime not a single church, not a single political party, neither a club nor a university faculty, has protested against what has been going on, as they did in every one of the other countries occupied by Hitler. There is no doubt that many were horrified by the atrocities first at home and then all over Europe; but no one dared say so. As far as we know, the overwhelming majority of the one or two hundred thousand Germans who may be behind barbed wire today are victims of denunciations for such offenses as listening to foreign broadcasts or some critical remark in public; judged by all available evidence, the number of people who suffer for having really spoken out what they held to be true must be very small indeed.

Reports on a German underground lack all confirmation. While steady news has reached us of local revolts everywhere in occupied Europe, no such news has come from Germany. It is true that both Catholic bishops and the Protestant church protested repeatedly—that is, against State interference with matters ecclesiastical, but not against the criminal regime as such.

Indeed the Church of Rome was the first power to conclude a treaty (Concordat) with Hitler. Neither the Vatican nor the Protestant churches rose, like some of their individual members, to fight the Nazis. Martyrs such as Pastor Niemöller went to prison for their own convictions; others, like Cardinal Faulhaber, defied mortal danger; but they did so as upright individuals, and never as the spokesmen of their communities. Ideals such as are presented in the play *Watch on the Rhine* are but wishful daydreams without background in reality. A Christian fight against a war of aggression was always unknown in Germany. Shortly before his arrest Pastor Niemöller, a former U-boat commander, told an American that he would again join up if there was war with France. Some Catholic dignitaries, advocating reinstitution of religious freedom in Germany, pointed out that a Christian soldier was a better fighter than a man whose only belief was in the State.

The German war crimes have not been committed by one million S.S. men but by twelve million German soldiers. Who are the soldiers who had their picture taken, cigarettes between their grinning lips, somewhere in Poland riding a car drawn by ten bearded old Jews? Who are the pilots who in their dive-bombers shot at refugee women and children on French roads in 1940? Who torpedoed hospital ships? Who burned to ashes Lidice and St. Gingolphe, killing the whole population? Who has suffocated tens of thousands of Jews in sealed freight cars, and massacred tens of thousands in front of graves they had to dig for themselves? Who, indeed, if not the German people in arms? It is the same people that twenty-odd years earlier destroyed French cities on their final retreat and burned French forests only to enjoy the last moments of power. It is the same men, or their sons.

In perpetrating such crimes the German individual feels himself as an organ of the State. To be an efficient State organ means much more to him than to be a valuable individual. And this also accounts for the development of his peculiar "sense of honor." The German kills *pro majore patriae gloria* any neighbor he feels superior to. He has done so not only since Hitler but since the days of his medieval emperors. Believing in his moral right, coolly and without emotion, in deadly earnest, so to speak, he brings death to others—and, if necessity arises, to himself. Thousands of Hitler youths today, at the end of the war, will sacrifice their lives for the State.

But no matter how readily the German dies for Führer and fatherland, he does no thinking for them. What he really requires is not thinking—but enthusiasm for the world domination of his race, and his own passion to obey. Defeat only upsets the God-given order of things. He is likely to lose his nerve and throw in the sponge. But in so doing he knows, after all, it is merely an armistice he asks for, a mere truce. His son, so he comforts himself, will try it again in some twenty years.

7 THE PRESENT DANGER

HISTORY has rarely repeated itself as it has in this war. Today, as in 1919, the same forces are banding together to mislead the victors with falsifications and mobilize sympathy for Germany. If the victors are taken in again, those forces will once more betray them.

For twenty years German propaganda has falsified recent German history. But since the notorious Bund and other similar groups opened American eyes, German propaganda has changed its tune; now it labors these theses: (1) that not all Germans are Nazis, (2) that Germany is not alone guilty of starting this war.

In America, France, and England, where some people still harp on the illusions and failures of their prewar leaders, the second propaganda line makes clever use of this domestic criticism. In a long war, governments on the winning side are always under heavier domestic attack than those of the losing side; with victory in sight and the original war tension loosened, every opposition party is anxious to prove that it might either have averted the war altogether, or have done a better and quicker job than the party in power.

This difference is even clearer in the case where democracy is facing its very opposite—that is the German system. German passion for authority is so great that the individual German always blames himself rather than his government. The government can never be wrong! The British public realized and openly discussed the fatal mistakes of their Chamberlains and Baldwins, but people in Germany rallied only the more closely behind their leaders. And how little of that attitude was primarily due to fear of the Gestapo is proved by the behavior of many German exiles. These men even side with the native critics of their host, the Allied Nations—instead of keeping aloof from family quarrels, as is the thing for guests to do. While uncounted Americans give their lives for liberty, those men have the audacity to write on American soil that both France and England share the war guilt with Germany. Such stuff is printed in American-German language papers.

The "Nazi-not-Germans" propaganda line is even more suggestive. The Nazis, so it runs, are a clique of wicked men who have "overpowered the Germans precisely as they overran Holland or France"; the "poor, misled Germans" went to war only under duress—an enterprise they really detested. "Hitler is not Germany!" is the chief slogan, and it has a convincing ring. For if Hitler were Germany, what about Goethe, Kant, and Beethoven? They, too, were Germans. And thus the myth of the "two Germanys" comes into its own. Two important points are concealed, or rather falsified, by this:

1. As shown above, the true German intelligentsia has for four hundred years remained without influence on public affairs. The State remained aloof from the spirit. This schism has grown steadily during the past fifty years; Hitler is its classical expression. Until 1933 the famous "two Germanys" lived, as it were, in mere separation; Hitler has divorced them. His hostility toward spiritual and intellectual values has gained a scope and a blatancy avoided by previous governments.

2. Goethe and Beethoven lived a hundred-odd years ago. The great epoch of the German spirit, marked by Goethe, Schiller, Lessing, Kant, Humboldt, and the Seven Stars of German music, is past history. Propaganda uses these names as if these men had only just died. In fact, their epoch was followed by the period of Hegel, Fichte, Clausewitz, and Bismarck—whose idea ran contrary to the German humanism of earlier times.

For three quarters of a century the German nation, intoxicated with victory, has followed the path of conquest, and has rejected the humanist teachings of tolerance. Since there never has been an active opposition in Germany, and all classes and political parties have worshiped authority and bowed to power, at least to obliterate the life-work of such old-fashioned internationalists as Goethe and Kant. Of all the champions of the classical period of German literature only Schiller was really popular.

In the past hundred years the Germans have given a number of outstanding scientists to the world; but since their work has been fused with international research, their merits have not always found due recognition outside of Germany. Apart from these isolated cases, these hundred years have been a period of decline for the German spirit. Wagner, Nietzsche, Marx are the only names which still live. They finished their lifework before the Kaiser took over as the champion of unbridled German arrogance and of new world conquest.

In the course of the past fifty years the Germans have yielded their supremacy in music to France, in poetry and writing to France and England, in technology to America, in pioneering to Russia. All that they have given the world has been the art of warfare and of acting. "German poets and thinkers" are a thing of the past.

It is therefore a fraud to attempt to excuse the aggressions of Frederick the Great with the Ninth Symphony, the invasion of Belgium with Schubert's "Ave Maria," or Hitler's pogroms with Wagner's operas. Germany has always been bellicose; but not before the early 1890s did she develop into the great disturber of world peace. And this is the historical point at which her true glory began to fade—when the works of her greatest sons had become to the Germans themselves almost museum pieces to be reverenced only occasionally on holidays. Of all the arts only music survived; Germans can never do without that—but it does not interfere with world conquest.

The chasm between the arts and the State is also indicated by the conspicuous lack of such great battle paintings as the Russians have, and the total absence of battle music in German composing. The only really mediocre piece by Beethoven is his Wellington Symphony.

German propaganda is directed by pan-Germanists. These men patronized and worshiped the Nazis from the start. They may disagree as to methods, but not as to the final goal—world conquest. True, they have changed their tune since the German defeat became inevitable; but in so doing they are no better than women who give the slip to their wealthy lovers as soon as money runs low.

That kind of propaganda in America started in 1943. It is led by some German-Americans, some big businessmen, and certain German émigré quarters.

They are unanimous in asking for a "soft peace," German self-government, and a settlement according to the Atlantic Charter. Either for romantic or material reasons, the people who make up these three groups have an interest in the comeback of a strong Germany.

German-Americans can freely give vent to their feelings for the "old country." The overwhelming majority of them advocate a "just and decent" peace settlement. In 1933 more than twenty thousand German clubs, comprising from eight to ten million American citizens, declared their sympathy for the Third Reich. Until 1938 their papers continued to run enthusiastic articles on the new Germany. The editor of a leading paper reported about his visit in 1933 to the Führer, adding that he had promised silence on certain things they spoke about, and one of the headlines of his paper ran: "GERMANY BETTER OFF THAN AMERICA."

At the same time nearly all German-American clubs were asked to display the swastika, to adopt the Horst Wessel Lied as their club song, and to close their meetings with a *"Sieg Heil!"* for Adolf Hitler. Most clubs accepted. Thousands of American Jews who, like their fathers and grandfathers, had been members of German clubs had no choice but to leave.

Every Pan-Germanist found it wise to present himself as an anti-Nazi. Nothing is easier, nothing less costly in 1945. With the proper references to Jefferson and the rest, these self-styled "democratic anti-Nazis" seek to pull the wool over the eyes of Americans and conceal their true aims—rearmament for another world war—as the Germans concealed them after World War I.

It is often overlooked how little typical their fathers were of Germany; precisely because these men disliked the German way of life they left Germany a hundred, eighty, or fifty years ago. Very few among them, not excluding the immigrants of 1848, were refugees; practically all came here of their own accord, in protest against the military spirit of their native country, hoping that liberty would take the place of oppression in their lives. The sentiments of their grandsons remind one of similar feelings in millions of Irish-American homes: they, too, harbor romantic sympathies for the country of their fathers. This seems to be a natural reaction: Americans of Anglo-Saxon descent become aware of a personal stake in England's fate when England is in danger.

The German-American who traveled in Germany every five or ten years before the war enjoyed his trip tremendously. With equal pleasure he admired the cathedral in Cologne, the giant barrel in Heidelberg, the lakes of the Black Forest, the Passion play in Oberammergau, the Nuremberg toys, and the beer in Munich. The orderliness and cleanness of streets, the punctuality of trains made him overlook the eternal mounting of guards and goose-stepping. All nations have their hobbies, so he thought, and Germans have always loved soldiering. After 1918 he admired the quick recovery of Germany, so conspicuously different from "tired and decadent" France; he did not bother to search for causes of German recovery and French "decay." Americans have on the whole a wishful way of interpreting the German character; so a man in love with a light woman often comforts himself with the thought that sooner or later she will change under his guidance.

Certain professors until recently were fond of quoting Treitschke who, as far back as sixty years ago, recommended a Germanization of America. The Germans, so he contended, must remain German even as citizens of non-German countries; for "every time a German becomes a Yankee, human civilization suffers a loss." This was written long before Hitler's birth.

None of the six hundred-odd professors sent over here after 1922 are men of great scientific reputation. They are primarily propagandists. Most of them became naturalized citizens of the United States.

Let us quote a few samples of their Pan-Germanistic propaganda under the cloak of democracy. One of them declared at the Free World Congress in New York in 1943 that the enormous increase of the German birth rate would make postwar Germany the strongest nation in Europe; therefore German rearmament could not possibly be prevented, unless by a temperate treatment of the German people under democratic self-rule—which, in the opinion of the writer, was the only hope for a change in the spirit of Germany. The tie-up of a hope for improvement with a condition plus a threat is typical German style. "If you are not lenient to the criminal, his children will become even worse criminals!"

Another Pan-Germanist declared: "One thing, however, unites us—that is the love, the care, the anxiety for and the pride of Germany, the land of our fathers. . . . We are pleased with and proud of a strong, united Germany, whether under Bismarck, Ebert, Hindenburg, or Hitler. . . ."

A number of these professors still recommend as future saviors of Germany such notorious personages as Herr von Papen and Dr. Schacht. As it is, these two men have contributed more to the defamation of the German name in the world than Hitler and his henchmen. They have not served the Nazi party out of any fanatical faith—they sold themselves to three different systems in order to remain in power. Schacht has twice cheated and defrauded this country and its bankers: first by luring their money to Germany and using it to rearm, and then by "selling" Hitler to Americans as a "guarantor of peace."

Fifty outstanding Americans of German descent have publicly rejected the Nazis, but at the same time they have attested that the Germans in their misfortune and helplessness had been forced to accept both Hitler and his war under duress!

The second group which makes, or furthers, German propaganda today consists of some American manufacturers, their agents and followers. After Germany's first defeat their ranks were soon honeycombed with representatives of German concerns, whose top men, as captains of German economics, were at the same time arguing the impossibility of reparation payments. German armament patents controlled Allied defense production up to the first months of World War II. According to Louis Nizer, these contracts forced American companies to deliver to their German affiliates—and thereby to the Nazi Government—full information on such vital secrets as synthetic-rubber production. Similar patent rights enabled Germany to produce three quarters of the world output of aluminum; the ensuing aluminum shortage in American plants explains certain drawbacks of early Allied tank production. Evidence of this was brought to light by the Truman Committee and others.

The I.G.F. has long ceased to be a private company; actually its plants are German Government property. On the other hand, the American representatives of the I.G.F. had long acquired American citizenship. Thus these industrial cartels were the ideal setup for German espionage. Several German-born representatives of such industrial groups were convicted of criminal conspiracy in 1941. Only presidential action put a stop to the claims of the I.G.F. in a number of Allied and neutral countries that it was an "American enterprise." So great was the power of some ingenious provisions in the international contracts of Krupp and Zeiss that the Nazis succeeded for a time in considerably weakening American optical and machinery production.

Fixed world prices and industrial production curtailments make a profitable game; and the cartels saw to it that these methods survived World War I. Why should not the present American directors and agents of these companies be anxious to continue the profitable trade after World War II? Most of them are still the same men; they realize that continuation on an international scale will require a strong Germany. A few millions spent for German propaganda count little considering the stakes. Sons and successors of some of the very men who were taken in by the Germans after the first war seem to have forgotten the embezzlements and have kept up their contacts with the old business friends. Some agents dine and wine with German industrialists in the swanky hotels of neutral Europe; quite a number of German businessmen have discovered of late a passion for alpine flora, Nordic fjords, or Spanish-Moorish architecture. One of them, Herr von Schnitzler from the I.G.F., brother-in-law of the recently killed Field Marshal von Bock (war and chemistry are kinsmen in modern Germany), escaped to Spain with his private plane, and assured his old friends there that his chief interest these days was in the delivery of Farben to gifted artists.

The third propaganda group is dominated by ambition—whose vocal part, as it were, is softly accompanied in the orchestra by the romantic motifs of the first group and the greedy tunes of the second. I refer to a number of German exiles who dream of their former jobs and their one-time influence.

These exiles seek to make people in this country believe—as some of them may believe themselves—that the good, democratic Germany whose spokesmen they used to be is still extant, impatient to call them home in a triumph matching Victor Hugo's return to Paris, Mazzini's to Rome, or Lenin's to Russia. Their status as anti-Nazis and their early flight from Nazism are offered as proof of their position. The line between naïveté and cunning here is as difficult to draw as that between Hitler's own convictions and his play-acting.

One thing is sure—these men have a considerable following in émigré quarters, and enjoy much greater popularity than people who share my views. Of course promises to his audience of a return to a freed and cleansed fatherland make an author or lecturer far more popular than gloomy pictures of an occupied country watched over by the victors to prevent a third outbreak of militarism. These émigrés have surrounded themselves with gullible American citizens, have set up committees, and published manifestoes asserting that the Nazis, far from representing the whole nation, are but a tough gang which held up the German people and for eleven long years kept them gagged and bound. Once these gangsters are done away with, the "other Germany" will rise again, as the Liberals did in 1918. But this time they will be on guard; and, in any case, as befits a decent people, they will join the peaceful family of nations. But if the victors deny this purified Germany the blessings of the Atlantic Charter, of self-government and international equality, then "chaos" is inevitable and will lead to another war.

This group offers a common platform to Pan-Germanists and Weimar Socialists. The old advocates of rearmament who vied with one another in their clamor for a strong Germany (only to be displaced by the Nazis, who promised to do a better job) are again reunited on the saving island of America, waiting for the tempest to subside and allow them to return home, to begin their old quarrels all over again.

Why should a fairly intelligent exile, alert for his postwar career, be expected to act otherwise than to support the idea of a strong postwar Germany? In his heart he knows perfectly well how little chance there is for a radical change in German mentality. But a record of his wartime activities for the fatherland, how he did his best to distinguish (and make Americans distinguish) between the nation and the wicked Nazis, may be crucial in securing him his old job in postwar Germany, returning him to the Reichstag, to the universities, the newspaper desks, the theaters and concert halls; he expects this record to be asked for by his broken-down countrymen upon his return. Sometimes these people grow quite eloquent in depicting German liberty as a kind of Sleeping Beauty, ripe for awakening.

One former leading Socialist has recently said that he is determined to do everything in his power to prevent the German Socialists from being accused again of a "stab in the back." Instead of doing his best to weaken the Nazi-led German Army, this Socialist, driven out by the Nazis, is apparently afraid of postwar accusations "at home" of having harmed the German war effort. That is how sure these exiles are, while talking of a "silenced German democracy," that the spirit of tomorrow's Germany will again be bellicose and full of revenge.

After World War I German propaganda allowed a few months to pass before it started its new activities. This time the same quarters are becoming active again even before the curtain goes down on the great tragedy.

8 HOW TO TREAT THE DEFEATED

IT MAY WELL BE that when these pages, written in the fall of 1944, appear in print, the armistice will be concluded, and the Allies will rule in Berlin. The first disagreements—disagreements on methods, to be sure—will already have sprung up between Russia and the Western Powers. In my opinion, the Americans are the obvious mediators between the English and the Russians.

Wrath and will for retaliation will be strongest among the Russians, and alive enough in Britain—much less so among Americans. A withdrawal of the American occupation forces may well be the consequence of such a disagreement.

The following suggestions—I established them in principle as early as 1941—are directed to the army of occupation in Germany, some of them to enlisted men, some to army officers, and others to the various commissions in Berlin or their governments back home.

I General Behavior.

Much depends on the first attitude of the occupying forces. Contrary to 1918, when the Germans refused to accept their own defeat, this time their defeat should be driven home to them. Germans are used to overlordship; any attempt to approach them according to the

Anglo-Saxon concept of fair play would have undesirable consequences. The Germans expect a victor to take his revenge. Perhaps
they will expect Americans to be more friendly toward them than
Russians. But no gesture of reconciliation will be of any avail. Here
are fifteen rules for the American occupation officer in Germany.[1]

1. You are entering Germany, not as a liberator but as a victor. You
are supposed to govern the country, and you will not be regarded as a
master unless you are strict and reserved.

2. Never give way. Anything that is granted as a favor will be regarded by the German as his right, and he will subsequently demand
twice as much. He considers fair play cowardice.

3. Always speak English when dealing with the Germans. Many
Germans understand English, others will easily find friends who do.
As soon as you speak German you will be regarded as a man without
self-assurance, who is seeking favor.

4. Do not keep smiling. Never shake hands with a German visitor.
Never offer a cigarette to a visitor unless you know him well. To the
Germans you are the successor of Hitler and Himmler; they never
shook hands. The firmer your manner of speaking, the greater will be
your authority.

5. Always wear a uniform. A uniform is the symbol of authority to
the Germans who for three hundred years have been governed by
soldiers. In hotels, restaurants, and theaters always insist on having
the best rooms or seats. Pay the full price, but refuse to accept anything but the best. The more often Germans have to give up their
place to you, the more their respect for you will grow.

6. The authorities of occupation should publish their restrictive
orders along with a reprint of the corresponding orders which the
Germans themselves had earlier imposed on subjugated nations.
Surely the Allies will imitate none of the German atrocities in occupied countries; but, on the other hand, they should by all means adopt
some of the restrictive measures introduced by the Nazis. The Ger-

[1]Drafted in 1943, and widely reprinted since.

man children, who have never heard of these things, as well as the many German civilians who lived through those years without adequate information will thus be reminded that their present restrictions are but the consequences of German crimes.

It is not enough for the Germans to know that they have lost the war. They also must realize that they deserved to lose it. And only such a re-examination of moral values can make them search their hearts.

7. Be polite to German women, but never be cordial as you are in your own country. If you offer your place in a trolley car to a woman, other Germans will consider you an arrogant foreigner trying to teach them manners. Under no circumstances flirt with German women; they would think it their duty to betray you.

8. Give conspicuous preference to any German who has been in a concentration camp or who in any way opposed the Nazis and suffered under them. To him you may offer a cigarette, especially in the presence of a German of the other type—a former Nazi or a German who has not been in a concentration camp.

9. Give open preference to workers. You may even talk German with them. They will be surprised by and grateful for any sign of friendliness.

10. If you are in need of something—a new lamp, a car, or a plane reservation—and you are told there is none to be had, reply with an icy look and the comment: "It must be here by six o'clock." It will be there in time, and you will have gained in authority.

11. Make everyone entering your service give you an account of his doings under the Nazis and of his actions under the republic. Even in republican days most Germans, including Socialists, were in favor of rearmament and revenge. Only those who can prove their leanings during the past twenty years toward a spirit of European co-operation should be employed by the occupation forces.

12. Be on your guard against German professors who quote English or American literature and history, especially if they do so in English.

Many such men have been teaching racial theories for ten years or more—but even that is not so criminal as the sermons of revenge they preached in the days of the republic. Professors and "scholars" form the most dangerous group in Germany, for they feign interest in a new Germany, yet still mean to promote restoration of the old. Besides, a learned German always considers you an inferior—you will recognize that attitude in the amused smile which promptly appears at every tiny slip of your tongue.

13. Try to learn by heart a dozen or so humane maxims and verses from Goethe and Schiller—preferably containing some critical remark on the Germans—and make use of them in conversation, quoting in German. The German sees in you a strong barbarian; he will be surprised at that bit of German erudition.

14. Forget the American habit of meeting everyone in an open way. Distrust everyone, no matter what rank he holds, who has given no valid proof of his honesty. Then, after some time, the Germans will realize that under your government personality and character count higher than military grades.

15. Never forget that you are in enemy country—even when all arms have been destroyed. Hate and the will for revenge will live on in the hearts of Germans for many years to come. The only way to get along with the Germans is to make them respect you; and they respect nothing short of the strong hand of the master.

II Who Is Guilty?

Most plans advanced by American writers on the treatment of postwar Germany take one of two extreme directions; both of them are to my mind erroneous. One direction is immoral and unfeasible, the other ethical but equally unworkable.

One school of thought, followed even by some liberal writers, advocates complete destruction of the German nation—wholesale sterilization, forced labor of the entire German male population (partly in

Africa, partly among Germany's neighbors), and partition into a dozen or so small states. These are outmoded concepts of punishment—and unworkable anyway.

The other school advocates reconstruction of the "poor and innocent German nation" through its best elements, support of the "decent minority," democratic elections, and finally self-government.

A third, which in my opinion is the only possible solution, lies between these two extremes. Since Beccaria's theories on criminality and punishment first gained ground about two hundred years ago, civilized societies have discarded the idea of retaliation; since then the punishment of criminals has been based on the principles of the protection of society and the re-education of criminal individuals. Surely the punishment of a whole nation can be based only on these principles.

Total retaliation is impossible unless the victors ascertain the number of civilians killed (said to be millions), arrest an equivalent number of Germans (as the Germans have done with hostages, Jews, and Communists) and execute them in front of their self-prepared graves or suffocate them in death vans. Unchristian as such a procedure is, it might be understandable if, for instance, the Czechs picked three hundred prisoners and shot them in the ruins of Lidice, where the Germans murdered three hundred innocent citizens three years ago. The Germans who committed that ghastly crime were driven not only by the orders they received.

But it is equally impossible to leave the education of the corrupted part of the German population to the so-called good Germans. Freely elected governments are subject to change. Twenty years hence a German government could again imperil the society whose protection must be the victor's concern. It is not usual to execute a previously convicted incendiary, but it is usual to guard him.

I refrain from listing again the thousands of individual German war crimes. The reader will find an excellent presentation of the subject in Mr. George Creel's *War Criminals and Punishment*.

The patient impartiality of the American court-martial which dealt with the eight German saboteurs landed from a submarine in July 1942 made a great impression everywhere in the world. The verdict which sent only six of the eight defendants to the electric chair was inevitably compared to German "justice," which had been killing uncounted thousands without even the pretense of a trial.

Russian writers who claim "an eye for an eye, a tooth for a tooth" have great precedents to follow; Homer and Moses taught this principle perhaps at the same time. Aeschylus was the first to dismiss it, as did later Plato and Jesus. Since then all Western religions have done away with the concept of vengeance. According to our code, vengeance is immoral.

Yet the question remains far from being solved. Attitudes of nations, or of parts of nations, still differ widely on the subject; they certainly differ under different circumstances. Public opinion in England unanimously attacked the bishop who wanted German cities spared the horrors of war; on the other hand, many Englishmen may be counted upon to condemn as "barbarians" Russian soldiers who do away with the German assassins of Russian civilians. There exist shades between some British bishop's lenience and the lust for vengeance of the Russian fighter.

The attempts to spare the criminals are apt to offend the sense of justice in morally balanced contemporaries, and drive their sympathies toward Russia. Tolstoy and Ehrenburg who ask for full retaliation are at least the spokesmen of a cruelly mutilated nation.

III War Criminals.

The trials against surviving Nazi chieftains are clear; in such cases the verdict antedates the trial, since evidence is before the world's eyes. An actual capture of Hitler—which is unlikely enough—would merely give a brief satisfaction to the curiosity of the public. Perhaps the best thing to do with him would be to hurt him at his weakest spot—his sense of vanity; he should be confined under heavy guard in the company of a hundred innocent deaf mutes with no one to listen to him! Penalties of this sort would be far worse for him than any kind of corporal punishment.

General rules for the forthcoming trials have been laid down by the exiled governments of the overrun countries. An idea of truly Roman grandeur made the Great Powers decide to extradite war criminals to the countries where their crimes were committed. This was indeed a promise of moral reparation to the subjugated nations.

Yet of all people certain German émigrés dared to suggest that the trials should be held in Germany—another trap, on the pattern of the notorious Leipzig trials of 1921!

No émigré, Communist or Jew, should ask for, or accept, an assignment as judge over the one-time oppressors of his kind. Jews should eliminate themselves a priori from any governmental combination in postwar Germany. If some do, however, return to Germany under Allied protection, they should stay away from re-education work; they will only be laughed at if they fail, and probably murdered if they succeed.

In short, whether residing in Germany or outside of the country, German-born men should not try German war criminals. Only the liberated nations should do it. The preparatory War Crime Commission in London has reserved to its own courts trials of crimes whose locality cannot be determined nationally. As long as there is no sovereign Jewish state, many crimes against Jews belong in this category.

Arguments in favor of the "innocence of the German people" have long since been refuted. Since 1941 world opinion has gradually accepted the theory of a collective guilt of the German nation. Normal men will deny that a soldier is bound by duty to inflict wanton atrocities on civilians. An American soldier would no doubt refuse to obey orders to kill unarmed civilians. As to the legal aspect of the problem, it is well to remember that the army codes of all civilized nations agree on the issue. The German code *Kriegsbrauch im Landkrieg*

(Usage in Land Warfare) explicitly prohibits any harm to be done to the "life, liberty, and honor" of civilians in conquered enemy territory; anyone destroying civilian buildings or public utilities in such territories is declared a "breaker of the law."

These principles were confirmed at the Hague conference of 1907 by the German delegate Baron Marschall von Bieberstein as follows: "Acts of warfare are not subject to international law alone; there are other factors too. Conscience, common sense, and the awareness of duties imposed by the principles of humaneness will guide these factors. . . . The officers of the German Navy will, as I may stress, always strictly comply with the duties that emanate from the unwritten law of humanity." To realize the historical importance of this official declaration one has to keep in mind that it was made in the very heyday of the Kaiser's provocative rule, and at a time when General Bernhardi's teachings had already begun to thwart the spirit of international peace.

Thousands of German soldiers have murdered unarmed civilians with cold ferocity, with cowardice, and with the unreasoning obedience of cattle. But besides, there are war criminals in three different non-military groups in Germany who must be arraigned: banking magnates, industrialists, and philosophers. The notorious Dr. Schacht is far more guilty than some mere army captain—and much more despicable than even Hitler himself.

Trials against a number of German "philosophers" present greater difficulties. I am not referring to Fascist authors who, like Spengler, were merely nominated Nazis against their will; I am speaking of the big shots. A Rosenberg trial, for instance, would be an event of worldwide importance. He should be judged not so much for his poisoning of public opinion as for the lack of knowledge and of logic which made his work possible and furnished Hitler convenient "scholarly" pretexts for his crimes. In this sense, Rosenberg's guilt surpasses Goebbels', for he coined the fatal slogans, whereas the latter merely yelled them over the air. Equally arraigned should be those high-placed judges and jurists who soiled both their learning and their own conscience by supporting Nazi laws and Nazi jurisdiction.

These trials should be held publicly, and provided with as large an audience as possible. The only case thus far of a large-scale broadcasting of court trials, the Moscow affair, concerned a domestic issue in which relatively few in the outside world had an interest. Three different reasons support my suggestion:

(i) Protection of the court and the defendants. For example, if fifty Germans accused of burning and pillaging a Polish village were to be tried in secret, and just one were acquitted, every living citizen of the village would immediately insist that the particular soldier must be the one who burned his house, tortured or killed his mother; whereas by listening to the whole court procedure over the air, the people, having all the evidence, would be in a better position to distinguish the individual defendants in a reasonable manner. Without full publicity for the whole procedure some of the injured will never be satisfied; and only such large-scale publicity is able to protect the court from all kinds of wrangling and confusion, and maintain its dignity. It is indeed not too much to say that some of the judges may well pay with their lives for what friends of atrocity victims will call overlenience, or friends of the convicted overharshness!

(ii) Humanity has a right to learn in detail how crimes against humanity are tried and punished. These may be high-sounding words, but I think the cause justifies them. Indeed these world-wide broadcasts will tell suffering people of the justice meted out to their torturers.

(iii) Education of the German people. The Germans would at once question the justice and fairness of a secret trial. Listening with their own ears to the barking and whining of their one-time leaders, reading with their own eyes truth and lie from their faces in a newsreel will lead them to check their judgment of the idols of yesterday.

These trials could indeed perform a semi-religious function, similar to the effects of the Greek tragedy in its own days.

IV Disarmament.

This must be the main goal of Allied postwar policy. It is easier, not more difficult, if carried out to the last rifle.

The wretched spectacle of Germany's mock disarmament after World War I must, under no circumstances, repeat itself.

"Germany is the anti-Bolshevik bulwark" was one of the most fatal slogans of the last generation. Lord Milner, British Secretary for War, was so much attracted by that slogan that he asked for a preservation of the German Army before the war was actually over. Wilson was in favor of a German postwar army because he feared that a feeling of oversecurity among the Allies would sooner or later frustrate permanent peace.

One of the Allies has declared herself in favor of a German postwar army after this war: in November 1942 and in October 1944 (see *Russian Affairs*) the Russians said that their country wanted to destroy Hitler, not the German armed forces; "for every literate person will understand that, seen from the viewpoint of future developments, it is not only impossible but equally inadvisable to destroy all military forces in Germany." After studying the Germans for over thirty years, the complete annihilation of their military apparatus seems not only both advisable and possible to me, but also the very prerequisite of a solution of the German problem.

The German Generals' Committee in Moscow, which Stalin has toyed with and perhaps looked upon as a possible regime for Germany, is said to have been abandoned at Yalta. Yet it is probable that the Russians, while abandoning the generals and eradicating the military and Junker ideology, will educate German youth along Russian lines. Thus, without adopting a Communist regime, Prussia would be led into radicalism and German youth educated accordingly. A few years hence we may be faced by two Germanys, separated by the Elbe, representing different patterns of thinking modeled on the way of life of the respective occupying powers. Through centuries of tradition Prussia has become the most highly disciplined region in Germany, receptive to any new form of discipline that may be imposed upon her and she may readily adapt herself to the governing methods of Moscow.

Stalin's attitude is likely to increase the fear in Western countries of "future Communist attacks" supported by a "Red German" army. In my opinion Stalin cannot and does not think of a Communist world revolution after this war; he will be too much occupied with the restoration of his country, which he so brilliantly set on its feet after the revolution. I base my judgment on my studies of Stalin's character and personal history as well as on the history of his revolution—both represented in my book *Stalin*.

On this score, too, the Allied statesmen could learn much from the mistakes of their predecessors. Whoever really knew the Germans could indeed foresee World War II when the Allies in 1919 allowed them a hundred-thousand-man army and thirty-six warships, instead of abolishing both army and navy down to the very last man. Briand said to one of my friends, "I know I cannot prevent German revenge, but I want to stop it for the next thirty years." He was a great man, and tried his best to bring about reconciliation in Europe. But in the end his attitude proved to be wrong.

The "Versailles Army" of the German republic was—as Schwarzschild points out—numerically weak, but strong enough to form the nucleus of another great army. America, too, has built up a ten-million-man army from a start of one hundred and eighty thousand. What counts is the professional nucleus, the quality of its equipment and the training of its officers, no matter how small their number may be. General von Seeckt was aware of that fact: in his German postwar army every single man was superbly trained, and actually prepared to take over the duties of a commissioned officer. Every single company in that hundred-thousand-man army—"companies of tradition" was the official term—stood for one of the old imperial regiments, and thus organizationally represented ten or twelve times its own numerical strength. As early as 1923 General Morgan estimated German armed forces, including "free corps," military legions, and rifle clubs, as high as five hundred thousand men. The road from then on to Hitler's twelve million is history.

The complete failure of the 1918 disarmament is accounted for in three different ways: (i) its character as only a partial disarmament; (ii) the insufficient authority of the disarmament commission with its three hundred staff members; and (iii) the survival of the Prussian General Staff which, controlled by the old personnel from the same old families, was a virtual guarantee of new conspiracies against peace.

A total disarmament will be more workable. A physician who limits the alcoholic consumption of a dypsomaniac by cutting him down to two glasses of wine a day only asks for trouble: the patient will never cease arguing with him about the size of the glass, or a possible extra drink on Sundays. Surely he will cordially hate the doctor who forbids all alcohol, but he will recover.

The ultimate task is to break the German of the habit of wearing a uniform physically and mentally. The task is to take away all arms, as adults take away dangerous toys from children. The task is to free German adolescents from their aspiration toward military education which they continued to have under the Weimar republic. Both army and navy must disappear to the last man and the last gun and the last ship. Nor should any sort of air force be permitted, whether military or civilian. A score of civilian pilots could easily form the nucleus of another air officers' corps, as a dozen transport planes could become the core of another air armada.[2]

[2]In *The Control of Germany and Japan* Dr. Moulton and Louis Marlio make the excellent suggestion that Germany be forbidden to rebuild her electric power stations that an international company should be set up to purchase power in France or other countries and deliver it in Germany. But they are mistaken in suggesting that a board "of not more than five persons" would suffice to prevent rearmament. An army working in every nook and corner of the country would not suffice to detect every German rearmament trick. The German will be as inventive and resourceful as a lover separated from his sweetheart by a tyrant.

Furthermore, I suggest that the Berlin building of the General Staff be transformed into a museum for the portraits and manuscripts of Germany's great thinkers, authors, poets, musicians, and inventors. A special room should be used for appropriate lectures. And on the frieze of the building there should be the following inscription: "Here were engendered the two world wars which plunged us into disaster."

The War Office building, one of the largest in Berlin, should, if not destroyed by bombardment during the war, be transformed into a ministry of culture, the War Academy into an academy for peace, and the Academy for Military Science into a teachers' seminary. In short, nothing should be left undone to turn the vivid imagination of the Germans from one side of their nature to the other.

Production of toy arms should be forbidden. Children's flags, toy rifles, and helmets have done as much harm to the German mentality in the past century as real weapons. Neither should the production of hunting rifles be permitted, lest the Germans salt away a few million of them for *Der Tag*. What shooting equipment is needed for hunting or gamekeeping should be imported; foreign guns, duly counted and marked with serial numbers, should be rigidly controlled.

The police force should be foreign. What German policemen are necessary should be equipped only with truncheons.

Veterans' associations should be made illegal, as must all marching clubs in general; one must try to bring the Germans out of their habit of marching in military formation. No German should be employed in a foreign country as military instructor, pilot, or armament engineer. The generation of those who are five years old today must grow up to be twenty-five without seeing a single German in military uniform.

On the other hand, Germans must be taught to accept foreign uniforms in their midst. Since a uniform is still the only formal expression of authority in Germany, nothing short of foreign uniforms of all sorts will hammer home to the Germans the fact of their defeat. Then perhaps Karl will say to his friend: "Fritz! This time it seems we lost the war."

All this calls, of course, for an army of occupation. A tryout period of fifteen to twenty years is a preliminary suggestion. Besides the Big Three, all formerly Nazi-occupied countries should be represented in this army of occupation. Small nations, such as Greece or Holland, should contribute at least a token contingent. The Germans must be made to see with their own eyes what kind of people their nation has tortured, and what kind of men got the better of them in the end. The German must be convinced of his wrong, even by humiliation, and Germans can be convinced only through demonstration *ad oculos*.

But these regiments should not behave as considerate guests who try to alleviate the effects of their painful mission; they should adopt the pretentious habits of the former German Army toward the population, and in their maneuvers display all the notorious clatter of German troops. This is, I submit, the only way of commanding the respect of the populace—respect, not sympathy, will be the decisive factor of the whole enterprise.

Surely Allied troops will not emulate the atrocities of Nazi conquerors. They will neither take hostages nor kill Jews, neither sack warehouses nor rape women. But what they should do is to treat the population with cool reserve, and always keep them aware of the superiority of their power. It is to be doubted whether such methods agree with American ways; if this were the case, it would be better, in my opinion, to leave Germany's occupation to an Anglo-Russian force combined with troops from the small nations. Besides, the occupation army will have to deal not only with Rhinelanders, comparatively easygoing people on the whole, but with Germans of all kinds, and above all with Prussians—who, as Goethe so aptly put it, "know better all the time."

Postwar conditions are likely to facilitate recruiting. One hundred thousand young Americans to be recruited for a period of three years will do an excellent job. An equal number should be contributed by

Russia and England each—which would leave a smaller contingent of the remaining nine or ten nations represented.

When these lines reach the reader, the planned partition of Germany into three occupation zones may be a reality. The scheme, as suggested, fits perfectly the characteristic peculiarities of the different regions: Americans occupying West and South, the British North and Central Germany, and the Russians all territory east of the Elbe River. It is a matter of contention how long this partition can be maintained; in my opinion changes are probable. The first to give up may be the Americans, who dislike every kind of domination of the defeated.

One point is of paramount importance—total disarmament. The death penalty must be imposed on anyone secretly possessing arms. This is the only instance where the foreign garrison must try to produce a feeling of terror in the populace. If it is thus driven home to the Germans that armament is the only thing the world denies them, they can be expected to turn their talents in the direction of peace.

The occupation authorities will obviously need the collaboration of German citizens. Many Germans will offer their services, but all should be carefully investigated before being accepted. Even a hundred per cent anti-Nazi is not necessarily a help. Many émigrés are again prepared to protect Germany in spite of all they have been through under German oppression; many of the haggard men who leave Hitler's concentration camps will not be sympathetic to foreign rule. As Schiller said, "Not everyone is free who mocks his chains."

Surely there will be many excellent upright people among the liberated inmates of concentration camps. Many of them will be tired men, broken in spirit. The services of the best should be primarily used in municipal administration. German city administration was once among the best. Good helpers though such people may prove to be in due time, Allied officers and enlisted men should keep in mind that no German must ever lay hands on any kind of armed equipment. Even the most decent German—and though a minority, there surely are decent men enough in Germany—is surrounded by the majority, which detests all foreigners. For too long a time have Germans been taught that "whatever serves Germany is Right."

V Government.

Disarmament and occupation will determine the form of government. Considering the misuse of free elections and popular representation in pre-Hitler Germany (as outlined in Chapter 7) neither of them should be reintroduced in Germany for years. The same goes for freedom of the press. For the Hitler regime has hardly purified the German character; what sometimes may look like a change for the better is probably merely general weariness. Even a dangerous criminal coming weary and half starved from his hide-out, giving himself up to the police bruised and battered, will, for the moment, have our sympathy; but no one would plead extenuating circumstances merely on the ground of that momentary weakness.

In my opinion, occupation authorities are in for a surprise. Once the Germans are totally disarmed and no longer see any way of rearming, many of them are likely to change their attitude and try to befriend the victors. This approach may be sincere in many individuals, and will, in any case, contribute greatly to a growing understanding. Talented and quick of mind on the whole, millions of Germans will soon learn Russian or English once they have realized the foreigners refuse to talk German.

Germans should only gradually be admitted to public office, and at first in municipal administrations only. But every single such official must be kept under surveillance. If the city of Frankfurt should be granted a native administration again in 1950 on the 1930 pattern, the commander of the British occupation forces must still have free access to meetings and files. He is unlikely to interfere with petty matters, but he must have a say in others, such as public education. The foreign garrison is supposed to have both governmental and advisory rights, and at any rate must be in a position to overrule the decisions of any autonomous administration.

The necessary length of the planned occupation is a matter for discussion. Americans often exaggerate the probable period, adding that no power can be expected to police Germany for fifty years. I personally have in mind a much shorter period, but I do not believe that any period should be specified in the forthcoming treaties. The world situation as a whole and the attitude of the Germans themselves will decide the length of the occupation. Such an "indefinite" time, to be sure, is likely to remind many Germans of the equally uncertain plans for the extent of reparation payments after World War I, and grow to a matter of more or less general complaint. Yet the length of the occupation must remain flexible; for no one is able to foresee its effects upon the mentality of the Germans. And not before the world is convinced of a thorough change, whether after twenty years or thirty, can the army of occupation be withdrawn.

Women are a special danger. Contrary to most Nazi-subjugated countries, where the women have kept aloof from the conquerors, the Germans can be expected to work out some kind of "philosophy" which excuses or even advocates a more friendly approach. Conditions of twenty-five years ago offer no parallel; true, then the woman of the Rhineland (which was the only occupied German province) more often than not kept strictly aloof from the foreign troops. With the whole country occupied this time, things may well be different.

Marriage should under no circumstances be permitted. The idea of assimilating German women by marriage to their former enemies shows as little understanding of the German character as do certain plans for a re-education of German youth in foreign countries.

VI Isolation.

Germans should not be permitted to travel outside of Germany for about ten years. This virtual isolation is one of the purposes of postwar supervision. Since Germans, even long before Hitler, considered themselves the chosen people, they should be only too happy to remain in their own exclusive society. But above all, any duplication of the sad spectacle of German post-1920 traveling must be prevented. Every German manufacturer or scholar traveling to Paris or New York would again combine his trip with a bit of propaganda for the "poor, suffering German people."

If Germans feel this restriction to be an offense, all the better. Not until they realize that the world esteems them less than other nations for the time being will they begin to search their hearts and try to change. That is a principal part of the moral conquest.

Special trade missions or international scientific conferences which are in the interest of the victors will call for exemptions from the general no-travel regulations. In fact, three hundred lucky Germans who might be permitted to make such a trip would very likely be the object of much curiosity upon their return; such *rarae aves,* doves of peace that return into the ark, are better messengers of international good will than any large-scale student exchange.

This wholesale isolation may prove to have a highly salutary effect. Germans will not be in a position to complain of imprisonment— what German would call his own country a jail? Neither is it an asylum; for the German nation as a whole is neither "insane" nor "perverse." It is like a sanitarium which, under the supervision of physicians and wardens, promises full recovery to a group of weary people. No one will harm them. General rules will forbid them to kill their wardens. Everyone will pursue his business and his hobbies in full peace; talent and inclinations may develop freely. In short, the one thing such people may miss is an opportunity to leave the large, well-kept grounds of the sanitarium.

Such surroundings may well restore peace of mind to a shattered and badly confused people. They can study both their gifts and their drawbacks, and, renouncing their blatant, hasty ways, may indeed come to write and even to turn out some good writing—as they did before they prospered and grew arrogant. To me this seems as good a road as any to a renewal of German humanism. Perhaps around 1950 tourists will make trips to Germany as they now do to Bali.

VII Partition.

Most partition plans advanced thus far are based on incomplete ethnographic knowledge; suggested demarcation lines often seem to be drawn by unskilled hands. Experience at Versailles proved that no such scheme can be put into practice without the most detailed information on the different regional conditions involved. A non-German, even with much travel experience in Germany, cannot grasp these conditions (and the German national character as a whole) as well as an educated German.

The partition of Germany can be looked at from two different angles: destruction of the German *potentiel de guerre* (Allied security) and destruction of Germany's industrial capacity (protection of Allied markets). The second issue underlies many ideas on the partition of Germany. Security, the protection of world peace, on the other hand, can without question be more easily achieved without partition. A total, unilateral, and permanent disarmament of Germany, as delineated above, would exclude the Reich as a military factor without at the same time destroying her political unity. A breaking up of Germany without total disarmament will never make Germans into a peaceful people.

If the United States were partitioned into a half-dozen different countries by a victorious Japan, present sectional antagonisms would vanish overnight. The die-hard Southern colonel would suddenly discover his brother the Vermont farmer, and Boston aristocrats would be caught conniving with Chicago "plebeians." The whole divided country would feel a renewed national consciousness; the common history, the common language, and customs would suddenly seem of enormous importance. And from that moment on people would never cease to struggle for political reunion.

Now German national feeling has a much longer history; its origins go back to the Middle Ages; its fabric is made of thousands of varied threads, linguistic, historical, and cultural—which, summed up, account for the present German national character, whether we like it or not. The passionate criticism of German ways which fills half a dozen of my books proves that I am far from seeking mercy for them. But precisely because I know them as well as I do, I also know that a total breaking up of Germany would give rise to a nationalistic movement beyond anybody's control. Although they may be expected to grumble day and night, they will slowly accustom themselves to disarmament; but they would never accept the loss of their ethnic unity.

After centuries of political disunity the Holy Roman Empire of the German nation again became a reality a hundred and thirty years ago, when the old rivals Austria and Prussia united against Napoleon. Roughly seventy years ago Bismarck rebuilt the Reich on the ruins of the dilapidated empire. This was an organic historical development; historically speaking, nothing was wrong with it. Apart from great injustice against French, Polish, and Danish national rights in border regions—the Reich forced five million of them into its frontiers—the only regrettable feature of Germany's unification was Prussian supremacy.

The existence in 1803 of more than two hundred independent principalities ruled by kings, dukes, and church dignitaries found the world no happier than with the unified Reich of 1871 and 1900. And the historical logic of its construction is proved by the fact that the Reich has survived as a political unit three widely different forms of government. Contrary to Bismarck's apprehensions, centrifugal tendencies in Bavaria, in the Rhineland, and in Hamburg were not strong enough to override the general feeling of German unity after the flight of the ruling princes in 1918; even foreign support could not strengthen these separatist movements.

The Weimar republic was held together only by the Reichstag and the Reich cabinet. The twenty-two states—in the main territorially corresponding to the principalities of Bismarck's Reich—formed a union fairly similar in its structure to the states of this country or the Swiss cantons. Although Hitler subsequently increased the federal power, he has not succeeded in destroying all vestiges of states rights in Germany.

The plan to do away with Germany altogether, and to parcel out the country to its neighbors, makes the choice of those neighbors a paramount question. American friends of mine whom I knew to be in favor of such a scheme nevertheless laughed when I asked them whether they would like a slice of German territory themselves if they happened to be such neighbors. Surely Austria could not swallow Bavaria; and Switzerland would not accept a single acre of the German shore of the Bodensee. And no one can seriously conceive of the Czechs wanting Leipzig, or of Polish and Danish aspirations to Berlin and Hamburg. The English would not give a thought to a possible annexation of Hanover, in spite of the past royal union in the Hanoverian line.

A breakup of Germany would make sense only if and when strong separatist tendencies made their appearance inside the country after the downfall of the totalitarian regime. But there is no indication thus far that mutual regional antipathies in Germany are any stronger than similar tensions in this country, France, or Italy. There is certainly no genuine hatred between Bavarians and Rhinelanders, Saxonians and Hessians, or natives of Hamburg and Baden. Plebiscites would substantiate this statement, irrespective of isolated separatist movements on the 1923 pattern which might be engineered by certain groups in South and West Germany after the defeat. The small advantages to be gained, let alone the great risks to be run, would not warrant an enforced partition.

But the widespread hatred of Prussia among non-Prussian Germans points to a simpler and yet not less effective solution of the problem:

a partition of Germany into a "German Federation" (with the Elbe River as eastern frontier) and a "Prussian republic." The cause for the well-nigh general anti-Prussianism is the *de facto* subjugation of all non-Prussian provinces by Prussia, as gradually accomplished in the course of the past hundred and thirty years. Even before the unification of the Reich, Bismarck estranged great sections of non-Prussian German people; under his leadership Prussia swallowed no less than four German principalities or parts thereof, and thereby intimidated and deeply annoyed the remaining states—a feeling which strongly detracted from the undeniable satisfaction of all Germans at the revival of the age-old Reich tradition in 1871.

As it is, Bismarck was not the first to annex non-Prussian territory for Prussia; as early as 1815, for instance, Prussia incorporated the so-called Rhine province. Rhinelanders have been calling themselves "Must-Prussians" ever since. As late as 1900 I saw a sign on a Munich boardinghouse "Rooms to Rent, even to Prussians!"

Federal interference with state (*Länder*) administration was not much greater in imperial Germany than it is in this country today. But both Prussia's supremacy and the virtual enslavement of the other states seemed to be embodied in the right to declare war, which was reserved to the King of Prussia in his hereditary capacity as German emperor. As such he could mobilize the whole German Army, or rather the entire German male population, without consulting either the Reichstag or the other ruling princes.

Two wars declared by Prussia and lost for Germany are likely to have added flame to the internal hatred of Prussia. A separation of Prussia from the rest of Germany seems, then, to be both a logical and a comparatively practicable solution.[3]

True, Bavarians, Swabians, and Saxons are not less warlike than Prussians, as the long history of their conflicts proves. But the spirit of aggression, the will to conquer, the idolatry of the uniform, the

[3] I have already discussed this idea in 1939 in my book *L'Europe et la Prusse*, Paris, Gallimard.

conception of the army general as the pinnacle of education—in short, everything which has made the Germans so violently disliked in the outside world has its origin in Prussia. In almost any school there is a rowdy who eggs the others on to mischief.

By isolating old Prussia, that is, roughly, all territory east of the Elbe River, from the rest of the country the brains and the limbs of the German lust for war would be paralyzed. The Prussian Junkers still own those large estates in East Prussia, Brandenburg, and Silesia which were, and still are, the very basis of their power—an influence neither the republic nor the Nazis could really break. By breaking up these holdings and parceling them out to peasants (who, some hundred thousand of them, still live like cattle), two birds would be killed with one stone.

And it is time that the high-sounding names of German aristocracy disappear from German history. Those military aristocrats who since the days of Frederick the Great have won all the battles (though not always the wars), and, win or lose, have always managed to preserve their own estates intact, must be made impotent once and for all.

As to Berlin, this city is certainly both the least attractive and the most efficient in the whole of Germany. Its inhabitants are equally insupportable and indefatigable, and live at a quicker tempo than the people of New York. Many Germans called Berlin "hydro-cephalus." Some outstanding intellectuals and scholars kept away from Berlin as much as possible, and preferred a call to Munich or Heidelberg to a professorship at Berlin University with its notorious regimentation. To be sure those who wanted to make money flocked to Berlin.

A separation of Prussia from the rest of the country would serve the same purpose as a breakup into a number of independent countries, without at the same time causing nationalistic repercussions. It is the scheme of the "two Germanys" put into practice. For as we have seen, Prussia herself has made practically no contribution to German culture. Once set apart, she will represent the one Germany, while the remaining lands, though not representing the famous "other Germany," will at least be able to reunite the cultural values of the country.

Again, attempted enforcement would be folly. A positive outcome of any plebiscite is probable—faced with the alternative of belonging to the "German Federation" or to Prussia, the overwhelming majority of Prussia's neighbors can be expected to turn their backs on her.

The annexation of East Prussia by Poland or Russia is a foregone conclusion today; probably half of Silesia will be thrown in. Although 80 per cent of the population of both provinces belong to the Established Lutheran Church, East Prussia is by no means entirely German as German assertions will have it; actually great parts of her people are of Slav and Wendish stock.

The three historic provinces—Pomerania, Silesia, and Brandenburg, including Berlin—have a population of about fifteen million. The rest of Prussia—Hanover, Saxony, Hesse, Schleswig, the Rhineland, Frankfurt, and some smaller regions, all of them purchased or stolen at some time or other—will almost naturally return to their original union with Central or Western Germany. Together with those parts of Germany which never belonged to Prussia, they will form a republic, the "German Federation." The old Reich city of Frankfurt, for long years the capital of the loosely knit German federation which existed in the nineteenth century, seems to be indicated for that role again both by its geographical position and its fine urban culture.

Without Alsace-Lorraine, the Rhineland, the Saar region, and Austria, this "German Federation" will comprise roughly forty-eight million people—more than the population of Great Britain. A postal union, common currency, and a tariff union should greatly facilitate free traffic between the "German Federation" and the "Republic of Prussia."

The advantages of this solution are (i) the improbability of a nationalistic movement, (ii) the total elimination of Junker influence, and (iii) the impossibility of a future Prussian king or Führer again raising an army from the whole of Germany.

Only the Austrians themselves should decide on Austria's postwar fate. Looked at from the outside, her case is rather confused. In November 1918, except for a number of selfish big industrialists, all Austrian political parties and all German politics were for the Anschluss. According to the first draft of her republican constitution, Austria "formed a part of the Reich"; only an Allied protest prevented her from going farther. Twenty years later Hitler's Anschluss, brought about by trickery and violence, falsified the issue. Once upon a time a pretty girl wanted to marry a man to whom she was attracted. But her foster parents put their foot down. The man lost patience, and one night forced the girl's door and raped her. No one could blame her after that for now turning down the man as a husband. This is the case of Austria.

My plan thus foresees three German-speaking countries (as a number of different French-speaking countries live side by side, or, for that matter, dozens of English-speaking or Spanish-speaking states): Prussia, the German Federation, and Austria. In Switzerland, Alsace, and East Prussia people speak German dialects rather than pure German. Besides, the times of passionate language quarrels are definitely over. No one today finds Canada's bilingual system, or the use of three different languages in the Swiss parliament, at all unusual.

Indeed, he who still tries to give a political meaning to a language greatly misunderstands the spirit of the age.

Actually, the eternal language quarrels of the past were no more than a screen for power politics; and neither are our present-day dictators the first who have used or rather misused the "preservation-of-the-language" idea as a political instrument. A nationalistic education falsified the whole issue. In fact, many of the German-Americans who so ardently advocate a strong postwar Germany no longer speak German themselves. Their children do not understand a word of it—and though I pity them at times for not being able to read Goethe's poetry, many Germans envy them for being able to enjoy Shakespeare in the original.

That Alsace-Lorraine should be returned to France is self-evident. The Rhineland and Saar should be internationalized. Parts of Schleswig are due to the Danes, first because they are half Danish, second as a compensation for the German criminal assault on Denmark. But the Dutch must also be given compensations for thousands of acres of fertile land lost to them when the Germans cut their dikes, rendering the areas unprofitable through the flooding with salt water. An extension amounting to the size of the flooded lands should be taken from the west borders of Germany adjoining the Low Countries and given to the Dutch.

VIII Reparations.

Two lessons should be learned from the first reparation swindle: first, not material reparations but disarmament is the core of any German settlement; and second, no one should loan money to a defeated country in order to "enable" that country to pay its debts.

This time no reparations should be imposed. The essential thing is to educate the Germans by doing away with their megalomania. A success in this direction is of greater value than any amount of reparations.

To enforce reparations, German plants would have to be left intact, or even to be rebuilt. And with their industrial apparatus intact, no power on earth could prevent the Germans from rearming again. Experience in this country has demonstrated how little is needed to convert factories to war production.

Whether working for the domestic market or for export, the very sight of blast furnaces and running power motors would give the Germans a feeling of new strength. They would again become convinced that Europe's welfare depended solely on their brains and their work. And with that feeling once again in their hearts we could expect them to repeat the performance which started in 1922: first these "peaceful Germans" exchange smiles and nods, then they begin to talk louder and ever louder—and in the end they shout in indignation that so efficient a nation as theirs should be "enslaved."

Meanwhile a strong Germany may well have become valuable as an industrial ally to England, Russia, or some other power; no doubt her industrial potential would make her a neutral to be wooed.

America, with her traditional sympathy for any kind of industrial efficiency, might then develop again that peculiar mixture of sympathy and respect which is likely to grow to a popular demand for equality to be given to that "poor oppressed nation." It would be 1920 to 1933 all over again.

It is sheer propaganda to declare that Europe's economy would collapse without German exports. For five solid war years the world has produced what it needed without German industry, and why should the world not go on doing so? Germany does not grow, mine, or produce any kind of goods which could not be grown, mined, or produced elsewhere.

If Germany should be left intact as an economic power, it would make her the strongest European nation in her industrial potential. This strength, together with her longer working hours and well-known dumping methods, would be the direct cause of large-scale unemployment in the United States. Germany would thus be in an excellent position, through economic penetration and pressure, to prepare for the next bid for world conquest.

"And how about the Germans themselves? They are going to starve, aren't they?" appeasing sob sisters will exclaim. Let it be known to these delicate souls that in the 1920s Germany produced 90 per cent of her own food. As early as thirty years ago reliable experts maintained that a more intensive agriculture throughout the country and a breaking up of the Junker estates would enable a population of even eighty million to live off the country. The so-called "desert stretches" around Berlin and Hamburg could be transformed into truck farms through intensive agriculture.

Naturally vital imports, such as mineral oils, wool, and cotton, will have to be paid for by a certain amount of export. That export should be strictly regulated—if for no other reason than to prevent the growth of mammoth fortunes on the notorious Stinnes pattern. Key plants of the optical and chemical industries should be dismantled and transferred to the devastated countries of Germany's neighbors; the patents should be regulated accordingly.

The plan of the United States Treasury Department of last summer did not propose to transform the Reich into a "huge potato field," as German sympathizers called it a priori to discredit any proposed solution of Germany's agricultural problems. In fact, the Germans are by no means likely to starve in decreasing their industrial production and at the same time increasing their crops.

But two demands are paramount in the economic field: a lowered standard of living and the export of labor. Both points are dealt with elsewhere in these pages.

America's conscience has already protested against the idea of "enslaving a nation for generations to come." First, it is not a nation but only a small fraction of its manhood which will work in foreign countries. Second, only half a generation, not generations to come, will be put to this work.

Wholesale extermination of the guilty nation might be an understandable retaliation for a crime which has no equal in history. However, it would be unjust indeed to let the guilty nation go entirely free and not force it to repair with its own hands at least part of the damage inflicted on others. Where German immorality has destroyed half the world, moral objections are somewhat out of place. The Germans turned eight million unarmed free men into chattel slaves. It is just and moral to make them pay with their own hands for that crime.

But hope must be left to them. The Allies should promise them full liberty and self-government once they have restored by their own hands what they have destroyed. Fifteen years seem a fair estimate for that task. After its accomplishment, foreign rule, though not foreign supervision, should be relaxed—and thus a new epoch of German history be ushered in.

IX Jews.

Of all the national groups in Europe none has been dealt with so closely according to German "extermination" theory as the Jews, and none with such success. Perhaps not more than two million of them will survive the ordeal in Europe. Therefore the Jews have the greatest claim for reparation—where reparation is still possible.

But as the Jews have been the only ones of all those attacked to be deprived of their very dignity as human beings, they also form the only group of all the displaced people that cannot possibly return to their country of origin. The majority of Jewish-German émigrés have found some way of making their living, and are not likely to wish to exchange whatever security they now have for a life of insecurity in postwar Germany.

On the other hand, some German exiles have so little pride as to absolve the German people of its liability to compensation, and even declare that the German law which implies such a liability is void. Some of them want to go back; they are not "the eternal Jew," but "the eternal German." Hugo Marx has brilliantly refuted their arguments.[4] The truth of the matter is that the Reich *ex officio* robbed and outlawed a minority—in obvious violation of international agreements signed by the Reich. Claims for restitution will be made on the basis of these obligations, and, if possible, collected. The German people as a legal unit is the debtor of injured Jewry.

The individual Jew has no claim on the Reich; for the confiscatory law of November 1941 had the same validity as any other German bill. The claims of the minority can be raised only on the level of international law. According to the laws of most countries the nonresident status of the claimant does not impair the legality of his

[4]*The Case of the German Jews versus Germany,* Egmont Press, 1944.

claim. Moreover, most countries which have accepted refugees but have not naturalized them still consider it their duty to protect their interests.

Sir John Fischer Williams, a British jurist, long before Hitler made a fine contribution to the discussion on reparation payments. He upheld the collective responsibility of a country for injustice done to others by its government: he pointed out that this injustice must have brought certain material advantages to the whole population, and therefore a change of government was not enough to release the population from a responsibility they incurred at the moment the injustice was done.

Some people may remember certain difficulties which arose when White Russian émigrés sued Soviet Russia through American and British courts. Looked at from a purely legal viewpoint, that situation may seem to have certain similarities to the case of Jewish-German émigrés. But in fact it is one thing for a friendly foreign power to deal with a thriving new country whose regime, though born in revolution, has stayed in power for a generation, and a quite different matter to deal with a defeated enemy country whose people remain responsible for the crimes of their community.

All German-Jewish congregations and institutions are entitled to restitution in kind or indemnity—irrespective of all alleged bona fides on the part of the present owner. Individual German-born Jews outside of Germany should be represented by an Allied agency in the field. A good thing to do would be to send a hundred experienced German-Jewish lawyers to Germany with an Allied committee, and have them investigate all individual claims.

It must be kept in mind that even a full return of all loot would be small reparation for what the Germans have done to the Jews. One should not fear, but ardently hope, that the Jews will harbor a deep resentment against the German people for centuries to come.

One thing German-born Jews should avoid under all circumstances —return to Germany. More than four hundred years had to pass before members of the Spanish-Jewry community returned to the Spain which had driven out their ancestors in the fifteenth century; and they did not return officially until the old decree of expulsion was voided by the king. But if some German-Jews of today are unable to emulate the proud heroism of their Spanish brethren, there is but one way I can suggest to bring them back: a plebiscite of all German men and women on the question, "Do you want the Jews to be recalled to Germany, to be reinstated in their old civic rights, and upon their return to be received with full honors by representatives of the government?"

A two-thirds majority should be required on that plebiscite, for nothing short of that could be accepted as a valid proof of a change in the German attitude. The abrogation of racial laws by the classic first statement of General Eisenhower indicated only the good intention of the Allies. In case of such a German majority Jews who still love the old country could return.

X National Symbols.

A thorough change in the outward national symbols is second in importance only to occupation and disarmament; for such symbolism means much to all Occidental nations, not only to Germans. The virtual boycott of the republican form of government in Germany expressed itself from the start by a widespread contempt for the Weimar flag and an equally common adoration of the old imperial symbols, which permeated German homes, schools, and government offices alike. As late as 1927 I watched the children of the late Baron von Bergen, then German Ambassador to the Holy See, playing with a black, white, and red Hohenzollern flag in his embassy in Rome.

I am not discussing the question of the names of Nazi heroes on city streets and public squares. Public wrath can be expected to do away with the signs marking Hitler streets and Goering squares everywhere soon after the collapse. But what is equally necessary is to do away with the much-cherished memory of past military victories as expressed in street names. In 1930 I made a statistical study of Berlin street names. Of all streets named for persons 60 per cent were named for German emperors, generals, battles, and miscellaneous victory symbols, against 6 per cent for outstanding German intellectuals or citizens. Following the example of the Soviets, who have done a good job in this field, I suggest that though a few of the historic names may be kept on streets and public squares despite their imperial sound, most of them should be obliterated and replaced by the names of the true carriers of German culture and martyrs under Hitler.

January 18, commemorating the establishment of both the Prussian kingdom and the German Reich, should be replaced by November 9, the official birthday of the Weimar republic; Goethe's birthday should take the place of Hitler's as a national holiday; and January 30, the day the Third Reich was established, should be replaced by the birthday of Beethoven.

Not only the notorious Horst Wessel Lied, but also the two other national anthems, must be put out of circulation by law. Beethoven's *Lied an die Freude,* from his Ninth Symphony, would make an inspiring air for a new anthem; Schiller's verses, which form its lyrics, could be easily recast. A new flag, preferably a white one—a symbol which every child understands—should take the place of the three consecutive national banners Germany has had since 1871.

Freedom of the press can under no circumstances be restored in the beginning. Special agencies should take care of the enlightenment of the Germans, who for twelve years have been cut off from the outside world. In no case must they be treated with tolerance before they themselves have learned how to exercise tolerance. It would be senseless to reason with them calmly about their own attitude. The only means to impress them is authority and *Verboten.* Under severe penalty all Germans must be forced to burn whatever Nazi literature they own. Next to every official poster of the occupation army the walls should be hung with the presumptuous *Verbot* with which the Germans covered the walls of the invaded cities.

Particular honors should be conferred upon surviving anti-Nazi martyrs. Since the Germans worship authority and honor only in the form of titles and medals, the old ones must be replaced by new kinds.

Naturally all Nazi plays must disappear from the stage. But neither must Wagner's *Der Ring des Nibelungen* be performed any longer.

The return of all looted art to the countries of origin is not enough. Priceless monuments all over Europe, castles, churches, monasteries, city halls, and art galleries, have been destroyed by the Germans. Nations which have suffered such a national loss must be indemnified. I therefore suggest that all objects of art, such as paintings, statues, vases, and precious rugs bought by German museums in pre-Nazi days, should be restored to their countries of origin without any indemnity whatsoever for the German owners. They have forfeited the right to be keepers of foreign art. German galleries should contain only German works of art.

This is the only reparation Germany can make to the wronged nations, and the only present these nations can accept. All this should be done during the military advance. A year from now it would be too late. The problem would become the subject of endless discussions in committees and in the press. Half of the American people would be in too generous a mood. What is done now as an act of war will be understood and approved by every nation. Just as the Germans are now dismantling the fortresses in the Po Valley during their retreat, the Allies should act resolutely as conquerors during their advance into Germany, destroying what should be destroyed, imprisoning every suspect who can later be acquitted if he is proved innocent.

The ground on which the victor puts his foot, the cities his hand grasps, should be held and used for reparations at once. Eisenhower has told the Germans: "We come as conquerors." Secretly the Germans admire these words; it is the only language they have been taught to understand. If the Allies wait for the peace conference to decide about Germany time will have neutralized public feeling in America and the original indignation at German crimes will have slowed down.

9 EDUCATION

No UNIVERSITY PRESIDENT or state board of education would meet an educational crisis by introducing the educational system of a foreign nation; reforms, however radical, would be based on American educational tradition. Quite similarly, my suggestions for education of the coming German generation are based on German experience and German customs alone. The Allies should no more try to introduce their own customs in Germany than an experienced colonial administrator would force his own habits on a Central African tribe. Just as no one could ever make Germans take their coffee with the main course, or eat mixed salads of oranges and cucumbers, no one could ever succeed in educating German youth beginning with the Declaration of Independence.

What should be attempted in German schools and universities is the revival of the best of the older German customs, combined with a strict elimination of everything that Nazi education has stood for. As it is, tolerance and the principles of cosmopolitanism were first taught in Germany at the same time as in England and France, and in some instances even earlier. Thus it is simply a return to the old humanism that must be the goal of German postwar education.

One of the first principles to be done away with in German school life is the military tone of the classroom where friendly relations with the teacher were out of the question. In the Weimar republic a small number of rural schools tried to introduce some reforms. These attempts could be the point of departure for postwar education.

Sports which in the course of the past fifty years have grown continually more military in Germany should be imbued with the Anglo-Saxon spirit of fair play. German youngsters must be taught that it is less important to gain honors at the Olympic Games than to understand and participate in the spirit of international co-operation in which they are conceived. The spirit of play must be restored to German games and their deadly earnestness banished. Mistakes are not laughed at, but actually punished on German sports fields; every boy has to stand at attention before the captain of his team. Actually, the German Führer idea is just as little a Hitler invention as the rest of his dogmas—it was in full bloom in the sport life of German youth long before the first war. In short, the continuous tension which permeates German physical education must give way to play, play pure and simple. Above all, German youths must learn to respect those they have beaten in a game, and keep in mind that they may themselves be beaten in their turn. This development of a concept of fair play seems to me to be the essence of German postwar education.

The Germans love arms as Frenchmen love wine. They should be "armed" like children who are given dull knives to play with. Bows and arrows are the only weapons whose use can never have any military purpose; they should be given bows and arrows.

As to the flags they are so fond of, I have made a pertinent suggestion in the preceding chapter. In any case, the decisive factor in flag-waving is the anthem or chant which goes with it. The words of the new song should refer to humanistic ideals preferably by using beautiful old German verses, and there should be no reference to the grandeur and might of the Reich.

Although uniforms are not unknown in some schools of democratic countries, they should be strictly forbidden in Germany. A sudden and thorough change of clothing habits is of the same importance to the education of schoolboys as a change of political ideas is to adults. I admit that classes in American schools sometimes look too informal to me—they cannot be too informal in the postwar Germany I have in mind. In Germany fifty years ago we youngsters were made to sit behind one another in a straight line—there were indeed rigid regulations even as to what to do with our hands in class. A classroom was like an orange grove with its identical products neatly lined up in rows for final processing—for we were educated to a fixed and uniform pattern.

At any rate teacher-student relations must be penetrated by a spirit of comradeship to take the place of the old awe and "respect." A transplanting of city schools to rural neighborhoods would greatly facilitate such basic changes; the discomfort of commuting would not be too high a price to pay for the effects of rural surroundings on the children—more salutary, I submit, than most of what they learn in classrooms today.

There must be nothing left in the curricula to teach German youngsters about German "might." Or, rather, the concept of human might must be cleansed of its connotations with national power.

Swiss schools offer a good model. No one teaches Swiss students that men are angels, or even united in brotherly love. Emphasis is put on Swiss peculiarities. The patriotism of small nations seems to be greater than that of people in big countries, and the Swiss are very jealous of their national liberties.

In no case should German children be robbed of their patriotism. They should learn the old songs of their ancestors which still praise the beauties of their homeland—but not its power—and which their fathers forgot for all the marching tunes they have sung. It will not be easy to make them understand why they no longer are entitled to defend this homeland. But by bringing home to German youth that their peculiar national status is the penalty for their own fathers' mistakes they might be taught to overcome a feeling of resentment and even hate in the face of foreign soldiers and the pictorial proofs of the armament of foreign nations.

To achieve these results, education should begin with the five-year-old. No one can save the Hitler youth of today, the boys of fourteen. But starting with the five-year-old an education period of fifteen years should be sufficient. Youth can be molded easily; the German youngsters nurtured by humanism in philosophy and history—and by humanism alone—will take to it within fifteen years exactly as Russian adolescents accepted Lenin's and Stalin's teachings, or the German boys themselves the infamous Nazi education. The enthusiasm of present-day Russian youth for their way of life is a clear proof that the re-education of a new generation is not an impossible enterprise. Indeed, if the education of millions of Russian peasant boys and girls into Communists worked out as successfully as it did, the transformation of obedient German subjects into sincere democrats should not be impossible either.

The first opportunity was lost, because after World War I the whole nation, including teachers, denied both war guilt and defeat. The victors paid no attention to the issue of education even when the revengefully nationalistic attitude of German professors became a matter of public knowledge. So German youth took the same road which their fathers had trod, and adolescents looked for honors in paramilitary formations rather than in sports or scholastic examinations.

This time the victors will be in the field themselves; they can prevent a repetition of that fatal error. A special Allied commission should be set up, to despatch two resident members to every high school, but five to every college or university. Control by such resident members must amount to full and steady active collaboration; in the case, for instance, of a history teacher becoming nationalistic in his lectures, the lecture should be interrupted on the spot, the teacher given a warning, and, in case of repetition, dismissed. Textbooks must be subject to approval by the commission, and should be studied for their effect on the students. Members of the commission should be able to read German fluently, but must not necessarily be able to lecture in German. Their task is not to gain sympathies for themselves and their country with German students, but to command the respect of German teachers. And the German respects only a man he dreads.

Foreigners should not be teachers; their accent would make youngsters laugh—quite apart from such subtle knowledge of the German character as is necessary in this job and cannot possibly be at a foreigner's disposal. In my opinion, the fifty thousand elementary and high-school teachers needed for the school life of a nation of sixty million can still be found among decent and democratic-minded fairly young men and women in Germany. Concentration-camp experiences should not be one of the prerequisites for the job, but everyone applying for it must prove his or her aversion in the past to everything that Nazism and reaction stood for.

The selection of university professors will be a more thorny question. Perhaps German universities will have to close down for a half year or so in the beginning. Of about five thousand German university teachers, only medical professors and scientists (except racist anthropologists) can be called clean of the Nazi stain. Neither mercy nor thrift should interfere with the necessary purge of the rest. The dismissal of four thousand university teachers to be paid a pension of five thousand marks each (as a reward for their no longer corrupting the spirit of German students) calls for an appropriation of five million dollars a year. With these men having an average age of forty years today, this financial obligation will cease in thirty years; thus with the death of the last man who lectured under Hitler the whole cost of the university purge would not go beyond a hundred million dollars—or about the cost of one week of modern warfare!

The new men and the new order must be ushered in with a rigid abolition of a certain set of university customs. Dueling should not only be outlawed but also ridiculed. Dueling scars, which are still an asset in application for higher administrative office in Germany, must henceforth disqualify any candidate. The beer-drinking contest, often a condition of fraternity membership, must disappear altogether.

The caste, or rather hierarchical, system which labels students according to their membership in an "elegant" or a less swanky fraternity must be broken, and all students put on the same footing. Not inherited titles, but learning and behavior on the campus should determine the rating of a student.

Sending a few thousand German students to foreign schools again will not do. After the first war most of these German exchange students used their foreign fellowships for making German propaganda, or—as in the case of Norway—coming back, gun in hand.

Geography and history should be taught together, both according to completely novel standards. The essential thing is the spirit of international co-operation which must determine both. German history must be taught as a part of European history, which in turn must be regarded as a phase of world history. German and foreign history must be synchronized in teaching.

Such textbooks then, differing from texts still in use in most countries, would introduce the student to comparative history, which puts domestic and foreign history on the same level. Both the commendable points in foreign history and the dark pages of domestic history would have their fair place in such presentations. In short, history should be taught as Rembrandt painted his portraits: light and shadows having the same value.

Most textbooks isolate domestic history and present it *sub rosa*— particularly in its clashes with foreign history. More or less common though this system has been in Europe, it was nowhere so strongly adhered to as in Germany. Since nearly all universities were government-owned, and all university teachers paid first by kings and ruling princes and later by the State, their faculties were entirely dependent on their exalted patrons; they did not dare to write or teach the truth about the follies and crimes of royal ancestors or the ruling classes.

To start the new teaching of history with Hitler instead of Adam would be the simplest method. Only by presenting to German youth the originators of their national humiliation will educators succeed in making them understand disarmament, forced labor, and international inequality. After the first defeat German children were taught to look upon yesterday's kings and generals as heroes who fell victims to a treacherous, materially superior world; this time they must grasp the scope of their fathers' guilt: they must be made to realize that

their fathers challenged the world, enslaved the Continent, and de-
famed the German name by unheard-of crimes. Germany's shame
must be hammered home to them.

In schools and universities, on the stage and on the screen, German
atrocities of both world wars should be shown to the youngsters;
they should see with their own eyes the causes of their national disaster. Thus they may come to wonder whether blind obedience to the
powers that be pays in the end. In no case must the great Nazi fraud
be covered up, as was done with the record of World War I. The
whole crime should be laid bare. Disagreements between school and
home are likely to spring up on that score; for only a part of the older
generation will accept the new teaching of history as truth, and adults
should not be forced into classrooms or movies which demonstrate
German misdeeds. Many German children have turned their backs on
their non-Nazi parents under the Nazi regime; the new educators
will have to run the risk of another wave of estrangement between
parents and children—but this time for Germany's good. In twenty
years the German youngster should be more advanced and a better
European than his father.

Starting with recent German crimes, the history course should follow
historic events backward; and in covering a period of five hundred
years trace all the selfishness, megalomania, and cynicism of German
dynasties, not without laying due stress on exceptions.

Allied authorities should not, however, import to Germany a translation of a world history written by non-Germans. Since a new textbook
will be urgently needed, the authorities should soon after their entry
in Germany open a prize contest for a world history written by a German. This would give the Allies the unequivocal leadership of the new
German intelligentsia, and at the same time constitute a proof of their
generosity in victory. Germans should not act as judges in this contest.
By choosing a history textbook written in the spirit of international
co-operation the judges will indicate to the new generation the right
direction.

In German classrooms the history of German wars and foreign affairs has always taken up 80 per cent of the time available; now the proportion must be reversed, and the same amount of time given to civic and intellectual history—yesterday's Cinderella. What efforts and time we of the older generation had to put into the names and dates of battles, dynasties, alliances, and successions of German royalty must henceforth be put into cultural history. In the field of German cultural history the German student may still feel proud of his ancestors.

Just as my generation was reared in nationalistic arrogance and educated for the worship of the uniform and the deification of violence, the new generation can and must be instilled with the German spirit of the great days of old. The period from 1750 to 1850 is particularly suited for laying the fundamentals for such a revival. It must continuously be pointed out that Germany has a double history brought about by the schism between Spirit and State, and the knowledge of this split and its interpretation will be of greater value to postwar teaching than the importation of foreign thought to Germany.

German students are more likely to accept the truth from the hands of Schiller or Lessing than from the books of Emerson and Spencer. As it is, the German soil is rich enough in intellectual raw materials to build a new temple for a modern generation. Goethe, Schiller, Lessing, Kant, Herder, Humboldt, Beethoven, and their twentieth-century successors—these are the destined educators of German youth.

None is more suited for the task than Goethe. He was deeply imbued with the spirit of the morrow, while the spirit of his own age prevented him from putting his ideas into practice as a statesman. As early as 1780 he wanted to see certain class prerogatives abolished; he believed that talent and efficiency, not birth, should decide government assignments. True, he was not what is commonly known as a democrat; he was much more than that. Once he said that the lower class was in fact the upper class before the face of God—which reminds one of Lincoln's famous remark that the common people were really God's favored children because He created so many of them.

In Goethe German students will recognize the great source of their new curriculum and its spirit. His life will teach them realism in thought and idealism in action. His work will show them hatred of violence and love of tolerance. Goethe despised and ridiculed the nonsense of war, and the complacency of cheap patriotism and national pride. German students must learn by heart the verses by which Goethe's Faust bids good-by to the world:

> *"Yes, now this thought shall have my whole allegiance,*
> *This word high-throwing wisdom knows for true,*
> *That only he deserves his life, his freedom,*
> *Who wins them every day anew."*

Goethe's bitter criticism of the Germans will have a most salutary effect upon students. They will encounter in his work the ideas of international brotherhood and the society of nations, both so foreign to their own mentality. In short, Goethe's life and work can be counted upon to teach German postwar students more than the history of all the German kings and wars.

German philosophy, writing, poetry, and music can thus form the basis of the new education. Even the nonsensical racist theories of Nazi Germany can be refuted on the strength of the work of German anthropologists.

In synchronizing the teaching of German history with that of foreign history, the student will come to realize that aggrandizement of power in Germany has weakened her culture. But he will find this to be a peculiar German phenomenon, whereas such imperialistic epochs as the reign of the Roi Soleil or Queen Elizabeth, far from hurting philosophy and the arts, led both to flower the more.

Students must grow familiar with the historic importance of revolutions as opposed to the fatal consequences of prolonged obedience to the so-called legitimate powers.

That most of the great composers of the world were German by birth—this the students should not have to learn; they have always known it. But side by side with that fact they must learn henceforth of the superiority of Italian and French painting, English and French philosophy, and American technology. Thus they might be led back to Goethe's wisdom again; he once said that science is like a great fugue combining the voices of all nations. Indeed, Germans must cease imagining themselves soloists and learn to regard themselves as members of one orchestra under the baton of an unknown God.

Another main point of the new education is tolerance. Tolerance is the counterpart, if not actually the sum total, of the sense of responsibility and fair play. As such, it should be in the curriculum of universities.

The lack of tolerance in Germany began long before Hitler. He is but the most perfect expression of the presumptuous German spirit of moral and intellectual self-isolation, which takes for granted the utter submission of everything and everybody non-German.

Now German youth must learn the opposite attitude: tolerance toward both the nearest and the farthest of men. Many people besides the Germans are convinced of their own superiority, but so long as this idea is not aggressive, it merely works as the motor of domestic ambition and competitive spirit, and harms no one.

Tolerance must be taught both in theory and practice, as both the theory of the master race and military training were taught under the Nazis.

Fifty years ago the great German drama of tolerance, Lessing's *Nathan the Wise*—which teaches the equal value of three religions—was still read and performed in Germany. The German youth should learn this great Song of Tolerance by heart. Of similar importance in that direction are Schiller's plays, *Don Carlos* and *Wilhelm Tell* —each in its way showing the revolt of thinking and popular feeling against hereditary tyranny; and Goethe's *Iphigenia,* the portrayal of mutual tolerance between guest and host.

Beethoven, too, belongs to these educators of Germany's new generation. He alone of all composers was a philosopher and a true friend of mankind. If the Germans had listened more often to him and less often to Wagner, Hitler might not have succeeded. Beethoven's *Fidelio,* the only German opera built around the theme of liberty, is the ideal feature for a festival the Allied governors may be willing to present to the German nation.

It would be a mistake to re-introduce German-Jewish authors to schools for no other reason than their having been banned. All text selections must be made only on the basis of artistic merit, and with the spirit of tolerance and humanity as a yardstick. In this sense, however, no curriculum would be complete without Spinoza, Heine, and Mendelssohn.

When I was a schoolboy, no German school displayed a picture of Goethe or Beethoven in its classrooms. Once I saw a bust of Schiller in the school library, but everywhere there were busts and paintings of the Prussian kings. The Führer's likeness which has meanwhile taken the place of the royal portraits will certainly disappear at the moment of Germany's collapse. But the victors must not leave it at that: without delay they should import copies of good portrait prints showing a number of outstanding men of German culture, to familiarize all Germans with their true national treasure.

10   THE MORAL CONQUEST

A NATION which for a century or more has been brought up in the worship of power cannot be subjugated by soft methods. Only by meeting the Germans as masters can the Allies hope to influence their minds and bring about necessary changes. Attempts at influencing them by an international exchange of students and scholars were an utter failure after World War I. Even the Quakers, who came as ministering angels, were suspected of wanting to "weaken the German nation."

The German takes generosity for weakness. Today he is again prepared to "organize the sympathy of the world" as a German Army officer put it after the first defeat. The world was taken in then; but its mistakes should serve as a warning today. A man who has committed a crime under some violent emotion may be brought back to his sense by leniency; but a previously convicted criminal who dreams of nothing but new adventures must at last be made to realize the impracticability of his ways and kept under restrictions and guidance until he is willing to change them.

As I have said repeatedly in these pages, Germans should not be "enslaved." But moral restrictions are indispensable in dealing with them. The Germans will never be reformed until they are rid of their *Herrenvolk* thinking and have been persuaded at last that their conviction of invincibility is false. The humiliation of the German soul, a deep consciousness of its guilt, is the only way to improve it.

The victors should keep in mind that no German signature is valid. No matter how decent and respectable the individual Germans who sign treaties and agreements in the name of their nation may be, nothing short of rigid control and the threat of severe sanctions will lend validity to forthcoming Allied-German settlements. Only commands impress the German. Once he mocked peace-loving democratic countries; now he realizes that being a democrat does not necessarily prevent a man from being a good soldier and strategist, and even a victor. General weariness and generosity of the victors bred the German contempt of the West after World War I—and this very contempt engendered the second bid for world conquest. To nip a third attempt in the bud is the ultimate goal of German re-education.

Enforced isolation of Germany as submitted earlier in this book would have the most salutary effects. For ten or twenty years Germany should be transformed into a virtual island with a foreign police force to watch over its entire life. But the islanders themselves should be free to follow their own pursuits, so far as their work to repair Europe permits.

That freedom, however, must not include freedom of speech. Germans should be free to listen to whatever foreign broadcasts they choose, and read whatever foreign newspapers they want. But they must not be free to print or teach anything without the consent of the foreign authorities. This restriction will be no harder on them than Hitler's censorship; in fact, liberty of speech and, above all, the individual responsibility that went with it bothered them so much in the fourteen years of the Weimar republic that they were only too glad to give it up.

The atmosphere of foreign rule with one hard hand and the teaching of tolerance and liberalism with one gentle hand will sooner or later prompt several million German young people to inquire about their own peculiar role in the society of nations. They will begin to wonder how they could find a more comfortable way of life, or travel in foreign lands. Then these young men and women must be informed that both self-government and moral equality with other nations will be restored to Germany once they themselves have rebuilt the Continent their fathers wantonly destroyed.

In my opinion, that time will come around 1960. A war between two or more non-German nations, however, would greatly endanger the whole program; for then Germany would become a potential ally to each of the belligerents. But with world peace preserved for the next fifteen years, re-education of the Germans could succeed. If it does, seventy million of them will return to the world feeling like Marco Polo on his return from adventurous voyages.

Then the Germans will enter a world of international security—and will begin to like it. Whether or not the world will like them depends on the attitude of the new generation. Prospects are good on the whole. These re-educated young men will be just as gifted as their fathers and less arrogant. Nor will they have spent those fifteen years dreaming—they will have participated in the technical progress of mankind.

The spirit of any community follows the spirit of its younger generation. Fifteen million German young people will do away with the ways of the oldsters, as Russian youth has done in the course of the past twenty years. Indeed, those who are five years old today may live to see, as young men and women, their nation's free return to the world—with all the historical virtues and capabilities of the German people.

But this time unarmed.